Study

Smart

Strategies

How to Prepare
To Be Successful
In College

Doug Stratton, M.Ed.

Study Smart Strategies: How to Prepare To Be
Successful In College

Copyright © 2018 Doug Stratton

ISBN: 9781521929193

Endorsement

Prologue

Being a success in college! Is that your dream?
Does the path to your future
require an education beyond high school?

Are you feeling a little nervous?
Are you thinking you could use
a few tips on how to succeed?

Whether you have already
moved beyond high school,
or you are just getting started

GET READY
to open a treasure chest of ideas
that are going to help you be
the very best student you can be.

The book you are about to read
is packed full of specific how-tos
that will help you…

Read better and faster.
Take better lecture notes.
Score better on assignments and tests.
Earn better grades.

In other words…
Learn more, faster and retain it longer.

I have taken my own educational experience,
combined with over 30 years of teaching,
and a master's degree in education,
to give you the best step-by-step
how-to-study-smarter strategies.

Whether you are just looking for a few quick tips
to give you that little extra edge,
or you are looking for a thorough,
comprehensive learning plan,
this book is just what the doctor ordered.

Let the journey begin!

Table of Contents

SECTION I
READY. SET. COLLEGE?

CHAPTER 1

Quit Thinking High School.
Start Thinking College!!

Whether you are just starting high school or already in college, one of the greatest things you could accomplish right now is the development of excellent study skills and habits. If you are a college student, you probably realize how true this is. However, if you are in high school, your greatest challenge in developing good study skills and habits might be a lack of immediate need. In many cases, the academic demands at the secondary level just aren't rigorous enough to force students to adopt many of the strategies that I will be talking about. Therefore, they end up with poor study habits and lack the more powerful study skills that will be needed at the post-secondary level.

So let me ask you something. When does an athlete prepare for the big game? When does a musician begin preparing for a major concert? If you are planning on going to college, then let that be your motivation to start RIGHT NOW developing the skills that you will need (not to mention the knowledge). Let me clarify this. College professors are going to expect that you already know how to study, and that you remember what you were taught in high school.

You probably realize that in high school you can often get by pretty easily. As a result, many students have "study" habits that are geared primarily towards *short*-term learning (getting a good grade in a class). But these habits tend to have little *long*-term benefit. Therefore, let me recommend that you begin developing habits which will not only result in good grades, but will also result in *long*-term learning. That way, when you enter college, you will have a stronger knowledge base, and you will be prepared to learn at the depth and speed that the college level demands. And when you leave college, you will have a huge knowledge base, as well as strong study skills, which should serve you well the rest of your life.

Let me add two more comments that might help further motivate you. First, how sure are you that you know exactly what you will be doing the rest of your life? Therefore, do you really know whether or not you're going to need to know what you are studying right now? Many times, people look back in life and realize the advantage they would have had, if they had learned more while in a particular class. This is true both in general areas of knowledge, as well as with specific pieces of

2

information. The difficulty is that you just don't know for sure what you are going to need to know in the future.

The second point is this. One of the greatest assets you could ever have is the ability to work well with other people. Anyone who has difficulty relating to, communicating with, and understanding other people, will find their opportunities in life much more limited; and knowledge is a big part of improving your people skills. The more you know about a wide variety of topics, the more you will be able to relate to a wide variety of people. So even though you may not like a particular subject, there are others who do. As a result, your ability to connect with these people will open many more doors of opportunity for you.

So let me restate this. As long as you are going to be in class anyway, as long as you are going to try to get good grades anyway, why not learn the material in a way that will make it last a lifetime, instead of just a few days or weeks? While you are in high school, why not learn how to learn in a way that will make it easier to do well when you are in college?

So how should you use this material?

Begin by reading Section I, and get to Section II as soon as possible, and start working on your study skills immediately. Do a little at a time. Start using some of the strategies immediately. Find out what works for you. As time progresses, get into some good routines using the information you are learning. At the same time, start looking ahead to Sections III and IV, and begin working on improving your test-taking skills and study habits. Then, as you get closer to actually going off to college, you will want to start looking at some of the chapters in Section V.

But of course, you never have to wait. It won't hurt to read every chapter right now. Then you'll know exactly what kind of help can be found in this book and where you can find it. After that, you can focus on those parts you need right now and reread the other parts later, when you need them.

You could also use the chapter headings listed in the Table of Contents and go directly to a topic that you're interested in right now. Although this book follows a logical sequence from start to finish, and you will get the most out of it if you follow that sequence, each chapter has specific information that can be used on its own. So don't be afraid to skip ahead to any chapter you want.

One quick word of CAUTION. This book contains a multitude of study tips. At first this may seem overwhelming, but that's OK. No one expects you to put every idea into practice all at once. Start with just a few, or even just one, and then add to it. And don't feel like you have to read this entire book before you get started. Think of this book like a treasure chest of ideas. Whenever you feel the need for a new idea, open it up and find one.

Let me close by making a certain point very clear. The time to develop a skill that you will want or need in the future is NOW. If you wait until you need it, then you will have two things to learn at the same time: the new content, PLUS how to go about learning it. Right NOW is the time to develop good study skills and habits, so that when the time comes that you really need them, you'll be able to concentrate on the new material you are learning, rather than HOW you are going to learn it.

Take a lesson from the professional athlete. Pro baseball has pretty much the same rules as little league. But any pro will tell you that each time they moved up to a new level (grade school, high school, college, minor leagues, major leagues), it was a whole new game. And the best way to progress from one level to the next is *not* just to be successful at your *current* level, but to develop the knowledge and skills that will help prepare you for the *next* level too.

Trust me. When it comes to learning, college is a whole new ball game. I hope that you will allow me to be your coach. If you do, I believe I can improve your training and get you ready, so that you will have a very positive and successful college experience. Just pretend that you walked into my classroom and I am your teacher. Therefore, each time you open this book, just visualize that class has just begun and you are ready to learn. Let the journey begin!

At this time, I encourage you to go ahead and read the

next chapter. It's pretty short, and I think you will find it interesting, motivating, and maybe even a little entertaining.

(NOTE: Even though I am using the word *college* throughout this book, the information and ideas that I am presenting should be applicable to any post-secondary educational setting.)

CHAPTER 2

WAKE UP!!

You're not in High School any more.

"Won't my first year in college be similar to just another year of high school?" FAR FROM IT!

It's hard to describe college to anyone who hasn't been there. Of course, every college will be unique, just like every professor and every student will be unique. But there is an old saying, "better safe than sorry," and that is what this chapter is all about. The likelihood is very good that when you go to college, you will experience many of the situations I am about to describe. The more you anticipate what those experiences will be like, the more likely you will be able to adapt to them. The fact of the matter is, college life can be so completely different from the world you are living in right now, that if you walk into it unprepared, you may find that your time in college is very brief, and not very pleasant.

"Oh come on, are you serious? Are you trying to scare me? What's the big deal?"

Well here's the big deal. A lot of college freshmen never become college sophomores. Many unprepared freshmen make terrible choices with negative consequences that they carry with them the rest of their lives. Those that do survive, often have a lousy freshman year, and find their remaining college years to be a frustrating process of playing catch-up.

College should be a wonderful, exciting, rewarding time; and it can be! But it can also be just the opposite. If you need more convincing, just do a little research. Talk to a bunch of people, like friends or relatives that have been college students. Go on the Internet and look up some statistics. Talk to a college professor or admissions counselor.

The main goal of this book is to help you be one of those positive statistics, not one of the negative ones. Trust me a little. Better safe than sorry! I've been teaching for over 30 years and have had many students come back after a year or two of college and tell me how right on target I was, and how thankful they were that they had been well informed. They knew what to watch out for. They didn't get caught off-guard like many of their classmates.

So what in the world am I talking about? Well, let me try to paint a brief picture of what your life might be like when you're in college. Let's start with perhaps the biggest change of all.

FREEDOM!!! You're not at home any more. No one you have to report to all the time. No one checking up on *what* you're doing, or *how* you're doing. You don't have to ask for permission any more.

RESPONSIBILITY!!! *You* are in control of your schedule. *You* get to decide when to get up, when to eat, when to study. *You* get to decide when something needs to be done (like laundry!).

Besides these two major changes, let me see if I can give you a clearer picture of what might lie ahead for you by simply listing a lot of specific situations you might encounter. Try to read through this slowly so that you can give yourself time to ponder how you might react to each item.

Let's start with dorm life.

> **A** new room, a roommate, maybe a tiny room, maybe lots of roommates.

> **A** dorm can be kind of like living in a hotel. What if you have lots of noisy neighbors?

> **A** party every weekend. (Who needs to wait for the weekend?)

> **A** new town. A big city. A small town.

> **AND** new things to do and see. A college campus is full of exciting things for people just your age and might be located in a metropolitan area where there are even more things to do.

Let's turn to the classroom.

Be prepared for...

Professors:

> **who** are extremely brilliant.

> **who** assume you remember everything you were taught in high school.

> **who** use a very large vocabulary.

> **who** write the most ridiculously difficult tests on the planet.

> **who** don't require attendance.

> **who** don't accept late work.

> **who** don't allow you to make up any missed work, even tests.

> **who** lock the door when class starts.

> **who** make all the answers on a multiple choice test the same letter.

> **who** give only test grades. (One class I knew of had only two grades in the whole gradebook: a midterm and a final!)

> **who** can write calculus faster than you can speak.

> **who** can speak for an hour without taking a single breath.

> **who** like to play games with your mind, your time and your grade.

who are concerned about their own research projects more than with your education.

who tell all kinds of stories that have little or nothing to do with the course.

who don't teach very well.

who have no sense of fashion, or that just plain look unusual.

who are psychology experts and love to psychoanalyze their students. (My psychology professor did this to me one day in front of the whole class. And I have to admit, everything he said about me was true. How did he do that?)

who enjoy putting freshmen "in their place."

who enjoy making you feel like you're not too smart.

who have weird mannerisms like they...

> stutter.
>
> never look at you.
>
> play with their facial hair.
>
> stare at the board the whole time.
>
> pace back and forth during lectures or tests.

Classmates:

> **who** are ten times smarter than you.
>
> **who** are ten times weirder than anybody else you know.

who are ten times better than whatever you think you are good at.

who have photographic memories (like the pre-law student that sat next to me in Freshman English).

who have very different habits than you are used to.

Classrooms:

which hold 300 people.

which have TV monitors so you can see the instructor.

which have totally blank walls and maybe no windows.

Classes / Courses:

which cover material much more complex that what you are used to.

which cover very abstract concepts that take a long time to fully grasp.

which have *several* textbooks (and you have to rent or buy them).

which don't meet every day.

which double in student attendance on test days.

which meet in different buildings. (Be sure you bring good walking shoes – and boots for winter.)

which meet for three hours at a time.

Now I know a lot of these things sound a bit negative.

Yet, I have no doubt that you will experience at least some of these; I know I did. I also know there are many wonderful, wonderful professors out there, and I'm sure you will have many wonderful experiences in and out of the classroom. But I also know that the admissions counselors and all the brochures and all the other advertising that you've been receiving have been almost all on the positive side of the ledger. But we all know that life isn't always positive.

So here's the point of all of this. If you walk into college aware that you might run into things like I've just mentioned, then your mind will be better equipped to deal with them if they happen. You won't walk into college quite so naive. You will have your guard up a little. You won't be unhappily caught by surprise.

Let me put it this way. If you are expecting the worst to happen and it doesn't ... awesome! But if you are expecting the best, and the worst *does* happen... it can be disastrous. You see, if you have this uninformed picture in your mind of what college will be like, but time and time again that picture is destroyed, it can have serious consequences on your state of mind. It can be a major distraction. It can lead to poor grades. It can result in depression. It can lead to people dropping out of school.

Again, let me emphasize that college can be a wonderful experience for many people. But sometimes it's not. And there will be some things in everyone's experience that they will not care for. But the more you understand this ahead of time, the better able you will be to deal with it.

Well, let's end this section on a happier note. Many of the negative experiences you have in college may become some of the best stories that you will enjoy telling over and over again for the rest of your life, especially in the company of others who have also gone to college and lived to tell about it. In fact, when you get to college, you might even want to make a game out of this and see how long it takes you and your friends to cross off every item in the lists you have just read!

So let's do this! Let's get ready to make college some of the best years of your life!

SECTION II

Learn FAST and FOREVER!

In the previous section I tried to give you the idea that college is going to be a lot different than high school. Perhaps the number one difference is that you are going to be ON YOUR OWN. This is especially true when it comes to learning. Most professors do just that, they profess. Many of them will assume that you already learned how to learn in high school; therefore, that's not their job. They profess what they know and leave the learning of it up to you.

On top of this, the difficulty and amount of material is much greater. And to make matters even more challenging, college courses move at a much faster pace, *and* expect you to retain what you learn from one course to another. Again, my goal is not to scare you, but to prepare you. If you are already in college, I'm sure you don't need any further convincing. But if you are still in high school, then one of the most important things you could realize is that *now* is the time to prepare yourself for what's coming. Put simply, if you want to get good grades in college, you will need to know how to learn a lot of difficult stuff *fast*, and make it stick *forever*. Developing college-level study skills is not going to be easy and will take time (and work). For the moment, let's not worry about *grades*; we'll get to that in later chapters. Right now we need to talk about what to do in order to *learn*.

Before we do this, however, I need to share a very important truth with you. Your ability to learn is directly affected by your overall health. Your brain is a living organ, a part of your physical body. In order to learn, your brain will have to make physical changes in its makeup. It will resist these changes (bad news), but it can make them (good news). The brain can store new information. It can increase its processing speed and comprehension capabilities. It can increase its memory storage capacity. The strategies in this section have the goal of forcing the brain to expend energy and resources in order to understand and remember information, and upgrade its capabilities when needed. Therefore, to do this you will need to give the brain the resources it needs: eat well (and maybe take a multivitamin), drink plenty of water, get plenty of sleep (like eight or more hours per day), keep your stress to a reasonable level, keep in decent physical shape, stay away from drugs and alcohol and cigarettes. Again, your brain is a part of your physical body and you need to take care of it. Don't underestimate the importance of this. Your brain can't perform at its peak if you don't give it what it needs. If you are in poor physical health, it's going to be more difficult to learn. You can't take very good notes if you can't stay awake. And if you are sick and have to miss class, you're going to fall behind pretty fast.

(NOTE: The National Sleep Foundation and the American Academy of Sleep Medicine both recommend that teenagers get between 8 and 10 hours of sleep per day. The NSF also recommends that young adults get between 7 and 9 hours of sleep per day.)

Let me give you one quick example of how you can put this into action. Washing your hands thoroughly and frequently is one of the best ways to prevent getting a cold and many other sicknesses. And we all know how poorly our brain works when we are sick. So... what can you do to help your grades? Wash your hands! Can you beat that? Think about it. It makes sense doesn't it?

OK. So you're going to do your best to take care of your body. Now let's talk about the mental side of things. As you approach this book, it is very important to keep in mind that we are all different, and the only way to know what will work for *you* is for you to *practice* the strategies that I describe. In the next three chapters I have a ton of ideas. Not every one of them will work perfectly for every person. Let me suggest that you try to find some strategies that you aren't currently using, then make some changes. Practice as many as you can. The more you do, the more you'll learn. Try to improve how fast you are able to learn. Get in the habit of doing a lot of little things on a regular, frequent basis. Make it a goal to find out which strategies work best for you, then make a habit of doing them. Develop successful study habits and get yourself prepared for college.

AND PLEASE, PLEASE, KEEP THIS IN MIND. I am trying to write a book that everyone can find useful. This means that sometimes you may think that I am getting way too detailed, way too complicated. If that ever happens to you, just skim through that section and focus on just those parts that you find useful. But try to keep in mind that there might be someone else who is thinking just the opposite. For them, all that detail may be just what they need.

And finally, let me make it clear what I mean about learning *fast*. FAST is a relative term in two important ways.

First, how would you describe your current rate of learning? Are you a *fast* learner? Do you see the problem here? Learning *fast* doesn't mean the same thing to everyone. So it is probably better to think in terms of becoming a *faster* learner. Therefore, I suggest that as you work your way through the next few chapters, try to look for ways that you can learn the same amount of material, but in less time. If you already consider yourself a pretty fast learner, then you will probably notice that many of my ideas are things that you are already doing. However, be careful that you don't read through this material too fast and therefore miss those one or two new ideas that could really give you that extra edge.

The *second*, and I think more important point is this. If you see yourself as an average to slower learner, then many of my ideas may seem like they are going to take a lot *more* time; and for some people, that might be true. But the big difference is in the *amount* of *learning* that is taking place. In other words, you might find yourself taking twice as long to get through a chapter. But what if you end up learning way more than you usually do? What if you end up understanding major concepts that you never could before? And what if you retain that knowledge much longer, perhaps forever?

In other words, I don't believe that there is some magical formula that will allow anyone to learn almost anything in no time flat. But I do believe that there are a lot of *study smart strategies* that will allow you to become a more efficient learner. How much more efficient? Well that depends on you, the amount of material, and the material's level of difficulty. Becoming a more efficient learner will take time as you practice new strategies. Therefore, be careful that you don't judge the effectiveness of a particular strategy too quickly. Give it some time. And then be sure to think about not only the *amount of time* you are spending, but the *amount you are learning*.

With all of this in mind, let's dig in.

CHAPTER 3

READ AHEAD!
and many more Simple,
yet POWERFUL,
Textbook Tips

One summer, while I was in college, I decided to take a correspondence course through the mail. This would be similar to taking a course via the Internet, but without any direct contact with the professor. A couple of weeks later, a rather large box appeared at my door. Immediately, I thought to myself, "I hope this isn't what I think it is." Sure enough, inside were 12, yes TWELVE, books. To my shock I soon discovered that I was expected to read all of them! And, in a very short period of time! The moral of the story? Learn how to be a FAST reader!

It's true. Many (maybe most) courses beyond the high school level will require a *lot* of reading, and in a short amount of time. Not only that, but much of the reading will not be easy. Both the vocabulary and the concepts will be more challenging. And if you are going to do well in your classes, then you're going to need to actually *learn* and *retain* much of what you read. Many students are going to find that this is one of their greatest challenges.

Therefore, let's begin our journey by looking at your

textbook. However, the goal is *not* to turn you into a speed reader. Instead, the goal is to find ways for you to use your textbook to help you *learn* the required course material, and in the *least* amount of time. BIG DIFFERENCE.

As you might guess, this is going to be a **BIG** topic. ["Why is BIG such a *little* word?" ☺] Therefore, I want to break things down into a lot of simpler steps. As you read about a particular strategy, I would suggest that you start practicing it immediately; you don't need to wait until you have studied the whole list. Then, as you continue to work your way through the chapter, keep adding to your "mental toolbox" the next reading strategy. In other words, make it your goal to develop a fistful of strategies that will enable you to accomplish the maximum amount of learning in the least amount of time.

Again, please be patient, this material is going to take some time to get through.

A. Syllabus

A syllabus gives you the details of what will be happening during a course. Make good use of this and any other course information the instructor has given you. Every time you get ready to study, quickly look over this material to see where you are in the course. Keep an eye on dates for tests, quizzes, and assignments. See what the next few topics will be. Keep track of where you are in your textbook. Always get a good feel for the BIG picture before you jump into the details.

B. Skimming

Glance over what you are about to read. If you are beginning a new chapter, quickly scan the entire chapter. Before you start a particular section, scan the entire section. Pay attention to pictures, graphs, titles and section headings. This is a VERY powerful step that takes very little time, maybe 1-2 minutes. It helps your mind get ready for what is coming, and perhaps even more important, it tells your brain what is NOT coming. Just think of all the things you could study; then think of your brain like a computer. In order to comprehend something, your brain must have the proper software up and running. A quick skim of the material allows your brain to prepare itself for what is coming.

Likewise, consider the alternative. We all know what it's like to just jump in and start reading and then a few pages later, have no idea what we've just read. What a waste of time. A little time invested in mental preparation is the BIG key to getting the most out of what you read.

Another reason why skimming is so helpful is that it reduces fear of the unknown. We all know that we don't function too well when we don't know what's coming next. We're subconsciously wondering things like...

1. How long is this chapter?

2. How much vocabulary is there?

3. Is this going to be a hard chapter?

4. How much math is there going to be?

5. Do I really have to know what's on this page, or is there something more important coming?

A quick skim helps put our mind at ease by answering all of these questions (and more). It allows us to get focused. It also does something else really cool; it creates questions! "What? I thought I was trying to answer questions; put my mind at ease." Well, you did. You got rid of some negative questions, the ones that cause anxiety and reduce learning, and you replaced them with some positive questions, ones that will enhance learning. What you did was create curiosity. Your subconscious is very curious. It might want to know what all those pictures were that you just showed it. It might want to know the meaning of the vocabulary words it just saw. It might want to know what the main theme is.

If you practice this skimming strategy frequently, your subconscious will catch on to what you are doing, and get even more prepared. Hey, we all know what it is like if someone whispers to us, "Do you want to know a secret?" We get curious. But what happens if the secret is really dumb, or there really isn't a secret? We get turned off. But what happens if there really is a secret, and it's a good one? We can hardly wait until we get the chance to hear another one, and another one. Your subconscious is the same way. If you get good at creating curiosity, and then reward that curiosity... WOW! Watch out Einstein!! (OK, maybe the Einstein thing is a bit much.) And don't limit this skimming strategy to your textbook. Use it on your notes, your course syllabus, and especially your class lectures. Learn to look ahead, reducing fear and encouraging curiosity.

C. Outline

Caution. This isn't what you might think it is. Please don't skip this step.

OK. So you've skimmed what you are about to read. You've created some subconscious curiosity and mental preparation. Now you're ready to read, right? Well, there are two more things that will greatly enhance your learning if you'll do them. And again, you guessed it. The more you do these things, the better your brain will get at doing them. Don't give up if you don't see immediate results. With practice, your brain will improve.

Let's do an outline!!!! (I can just hear all of the cheering going on.) However, this time, do your outline as quickly and painlessly as possible. You're not going to do an outline to please a teacher; you're going to do it to help your brain. Therefore, here's the good news. Do the outline in whatever manner you want. Do it however it helps you learn better.

Now if you love to do outlining, that's wonderful. But what I'm talking about is doing something that takes only about five minutes. Therefore, abbreviate as much as possible.

Different from any provided outline the instructor may give you, this outline is your own. And this outline is not just a study outline. This is a memory organizer. This is like setting up computer directories to save your files in;

so be very brief. Keep your eye on the big picture. The idea here is to take just a few brief minutes to write down the major structure of the chapter. Some people find it helpful and efficient to leave lots of space between these major points in their outline so that later, when they are studying a particular section, they can put notes within the previously made outline. Myself, I prefer to keep my simple, big-picture outline separate from my detailed notes. After all, while I'm making the outline, I don't know how much space I'll want later on for each item. Of course, if you are doing all of this on a computer, it's no big deal.

Now let's pause for a moment and think about what we are trying to accomplish, and why this simple step can be so powerful. When we read, we are asking our brain to analyze and remember details. If we do that randomly, what are the odds that we will be able to retrieve that information from our brain when we need it? But, if we take a moment to let our brain see what's coming, and how it's organized, it will have a better chance of understanding and remembering what it sees.

The fact of the matter is, our subconscious is actually doing this whether we realize it or not. I should say *trying* to do this. If the material is very familiar (You like Civil War history and you're reading about the Civil War.) then your brain can easily sort, organize, analyze and store the new information. The more familiar the material is, the less you will need to actually write down. But if the information is less familiar (You're not that up on the structure of the atom, and you're studying the periodic table in chemistry.) then the more *un*likely it will be that your brain will be able to sort, organize, analyze, and store the new information. Therefore, the more you can step in and help your brain, the better your results will be.

This is why when we just jump in and start reading, sometimes a few pages later, we have no idea what we've just read. The whole time our conscious brain was trying to read for comprehension, our subconscious brain was trying to figure out what in the world we were doing. It was trying to accomplish strategies A, B and C above: organizing, skimming, and summarizing. The more unfamiliar the material is, the more overwhelmed your brain will become trying to do all of this, until it has a core overload and a mental meltdown.

So what do you suppose happens to your brain if it has this negative experience every time you open a textbook? It won't take long before your brain despises reading a textbook. It hates the mental torture you put it through. Now, if you have already created this negative pattern in your study habits, don't cry! You can change!! But you will have to realize that it will take extra effort to undo the damage. The person who never had a secret suddenly does have a secret. How many times will they need to give you a really good secret to overcome the effects of all those bad or nonexistent secrets they used to have? Give yourself a chance. In time, you will see the change take hold.

D. Objectives

Never, ever read something without knowing *why*. That's what these first four points (A through D) should help you with. Clearly identify what it is that you need to learn from what you are about to read. Don't just read a chapter straight through and be satisfied that you "read the chapter." In fact, in order to learn something difficult, you'll probably end up reading a particular section many times.

So why are you reading the chapter? Because the teacher told you to? If your goal in general is to learn, then the answer to the question is what we call an objective (or a specific educational learning outcome).

So where do you find these learning objectives?

1. Instructor's outline, syllabus, class notes
2. Assignment questions
3. Textbook margin notes, headings, section review questions, chapter summaries

OK, I need to pause briefly and give you some brain theory. Your brain will use what it currently understands in order to try to comprehend new material. If the new material is very similar to what it already knows, your brain will need very little time to add this new knowledge to its warehouse. But the more unfamiliar, it will need more time. This means multiple readings, processing the information in a variety of ways, and other study helps.

Each time you approach the same material, your brain will be able to decipher more and more of it. And here is a big one. If the material is so complex that it is beyond your brain's current problem-solving capability, it will eventually put in an order for an upgrade. This is awesome! But it is not easy. You have to understand the tremendous request you are making of your brain. It will not take such a request lightly. To increase processing speed and power, to increase memory storage capacity, your brain will have to build a lot of new neural connections. You will have to make this request of your brain multiple times, day after day, week after week, even month after month. And you must give the brain the resources it needs to do this gigantic task. I mentioned it earlier: rest, nutrition, water, no drugs, and keep in shape. And you must be patient with yourself. Adding some positive self-talk (like: "You can do this, I know you can.") wouldn't hurt either. Your brain will resist this "upgrade," but with persistence, a positive attitude and time, it will give in and it will get the job done.

OK, more on the brain later. But for now, back to the study tips.

E. Don't copy

We've all done it. We've read a chapter, copied vocabulary, looked up answers to questions and copied what the book said. And what good did it do us? How much did we really *learn*? What did we remember a year later? So, don't read and take notes at the same time.

Instead, read to comprehend. Then, *after* you comprehend, write your notes. Let's take some time to focus on the details of each of these two very important steps.

F. Read to comprehend

The BIG key to reading comprehension is knowing exactly what it is that you are trying to learn. Let's take two examples.

Example 1

You're trying to understand the battle strategy of a particular general during the Civil War. You are already familiar with the vocabulary, the people, and the setting. You quickly glide through a lot of familiar material, slowing down to carefully analyze any material pertaining to the battle strategy in question. When you have finished reading the appropriate pages, you now have identified the location of the material that you need to study. You go back and reread just those portions. You contemplate what you have just read. You jot down any key points you need to memorize and you summarize the key parts of the battle strategy.

Example 2

You're trying to understand the organization of the Periodic Table of the Elements. You skim the chapter and it all looks like a foreign language. You read the objectives for the chapter and you're not sure what they mean. As you read the chapter, you find a great deal of vocabulary that you don't know. The examples the text uses are not familiar to you. You try to read, but you are hopelessly lost and confused. You slam the book shut in frustration.

Now it's clear that the person in the Civil War example doesn't need a whole lot of help. Or should I say, the person's brain doesn't need much help. This is true any time we are dealing with subject matter that is very familiar to us. The brain is actually skimming and outlining and identifying objectives, even when we don't realize it. But when the material is *un*familiar to us, as the brain tries to skim and outline and identify, it fails. Therefore, the student's real problem is, they don't see the *cause* of the problem, they just see the result: lack of learning followed by poor grades. By attacking the *cause* of the problem, and not the symptom, we can really help the brain to comprehend what we are reading.

So let me clarify what I mean by "*cause.*" When trying to comprehend new material, poor learning is "*caused*" by such things as:

  1. A lack of previous learning (knowledge of specific vocabulary and concepts).
  2. Insufficient brain power (how well have you developed the brain you were born with).
  3. Improper or insufficient preparation for learning.
  4. Poor reading comprehension strategies.

While it may seem that the first two items are beyond

your control, believe it or not, they aren't. The goal of this book is to help you improve in all of these areas, but you also have to be realistic. No two people have the same potential or past. Both the natural abilities we were born with and the mental nurturing that we have received, will play a part in where our current academic abilities stand. Some are going to have a lot more work (and difficulty) than others. But rest assured, everyone can improve. Many who thus far in life have put very little effort into improving their study skills, will see a vast amount of improvement as they put these reading strategies into practice.

So let me take some time to offer some detailed steps to help you improve your reading comprehension.

The first step is to carefully complete strategies A, B, C and D as I have just explained. In other words...

A. Review the course outline to see where you've been and where you are headed in the course.

B. Skim the current section.

C. Prepare (or refer to) a brief outline to help organize your brain.

D. Identify the specific objective in what you are about to read.

Good reading comprehension demands proper pre-reading preparation. Don't kid yourself. If you find learning difficult, you have a lot of work to do. You have already gone through many years of education. Part of that education was to prepare you for this moment. So if you didn't adequately learn what you were supposed to learn, you are now at a disadvantage as you try to learn new things that depend on the information that you missed. So what do you do? Well, it depends on the seriousness of the situation. Get some advice. How bad is it? Do you need to drop the class and get in a lower level class that will allow you to gain the knowledge that you missed? Do you need to retake a class? Do you need to get some remediation? Would a tutor help? Do you need to do some independent studying?

You can't escape the fact that knowledge builds upon knowledge. When your foundation is not solid, you will continually have problems until you do something about it. This is why college courses have prerequisites and why most colleges have some remedial courses in basic subjects. It is also why they have placement tests and certain admission requirements (like minimum ACT scores). So the hard truth is that if there are cracks in your foundation, you will need to develop a plan to deal with them in order to move upward. There is very little that anyone can do for you if you are in way over your head. My best suggestion is to take a step back, and get into a course that will allow you to remediate your lack of basic knowledge in the appropriate subject. After having done that, reset your future plans. I would highly recommend that you get lots of quality advice from teachers, academic advisors, learning specialists, fellow students, parents, etc.

OK. So let's go back to *Example 2*. Just because you don't understand the objective and there is a lot of new material in a chapter, doesn't mean it is time to abandon ship. It does mean that you are going to need to work harder. Hopefully, it will motivate you even more to use the strategies that I am talking about. Don't just work harder, *work smarter* too.

Here is my number one piece of advice for a difficult learning situation: Read, reread, reread, reread... "But wait a minute. What's new about that? That's what I do now and it doesn't work." OK. I hear you. But here is what you're going to do. You're going to read *differently*. And, you are going to plan **when** you read, *differently*.

To begin with, let me give you a principle to keep in mind as you prepare to read differently. Your brain has a lot of work to do, most of it at the subconscious level. Think of learning as requiring the building of new connections between the nerve cells in your brain. Therefore, because your brain is a living organ, the amount of comprehension that will take place while reading will be directly related to your overall health. You can't ignore this. If you are reading in the middle of the night, well... need I say more? Don't complain about the book, the teacher, or anything else if you are not willing to make some changes. Are you watching your diet, sleep, exercise, hygiene? And as long as we are on this... what about your study environment? Are you in a place where you can concentrate? And don't give me this, "I always listen to music when I study." If that is true, and you are making straight A's and you are retaining the knowledge year after year, then fine. But if not, don't fool yourself. If you are having trouble with reading comprehension, then find a **quiet** place to read when you are **100% alert**. **AND TURN OFF THE MUSIC!** If you don't make a *conscious* effort to make learning a top priority, your *subconscious* (where most of the learning takes place) won't either.

Let's review. Have you:

1. Checked the syllabus?
2. Skimmed the whole chapter?
3. Made a brief outline of the chapter?
4. Listed the objectives for the chapter (briefly, using abbreviations)?

Now, you look at the chapter and identify the first objective that the chapter deals with. (Note: this doesn't have to be the first objective in your list of objectives.) You may want to rewrite this objective (using abbrs. of course) in your notebook. Now thoroughly skim this section to clearly identify the beginning and ending of the part of this chapter that deals specifically with this objective. Under the objective, write down any details you notice, such as: vocab terms, names, dates, key concepts, etc. But don't write down any definitions or explanations; leave space to fill that in later. Next, read this section at a fairly fast pace. Your goal is *not* to comprehend the new material, *yet*. The goal is to identify what material you are already familiar with. So don't gloss over the intro. In fact, the intro may be the only part of the reading that is clear. And if that is true, it is all the more important that you clearly get the point they are trying to make. So carefully read the intro, in order to get the general idea of what is about to come. Then, read the section, slowing down a little when you understand what they are saying, and speeding up a little when you do not.

So what is this doing? You are building confidence inside your brain. You are giving your brain a chance to clearly identify what it knows before launching it into the unknown. This is like taking a trip. You need to clearly know where you are before you look at a map to get somewhere else. The key to not getting lost is always knowing where you are. (Wow, I sound like Yogi Berra. No, I don't mean Yogi Bear. Berra was a baseball player known for saying obvious stuff like, "It's not over till it's over.") When you start feeling lost, retreat to familiar ground. Your brain will work best if it keeps approaching new material while having a very clear focus on old material. This is why it is always good to review old material before studying new material. In addition, this means your brain will store the new info with the old, making it easier to retrieve the data later.

Now that you have made a quick read of the section, read it again. This time a little slower, and with the following two purposes. First: to reinforce, to make firm your grasp of that which you are able to understand. Second: to load into your subconscious the material you don't understand. Think of this like loading a new program (or app) onto your computer (or phone).

Now at this point we want to give the subconscious some time to ponder this new information. That means we don't want to start studying it right away. How long you wait will depend upon a lot of factors. Too soon, and your brain will not have had time to process the new data. Too long, and your brain will start to delete the new, unused data. These factors would include the amount of material, its difficulty, your natural abilities, the amount of other new learning that you are doing, and your health. In general, I would say wait maybe an hour or two, but no more than a day.

So what can you do in the meantime? Lots of things. You might switch to something totally different: study for a different class, work on an assignment, do some research at the library, eat a meal, exercise, or talk with a friend. The idea is to cause your brain to use a different set of nerve cells. Think of this like using different muscle groups during a physical workout. If you feel your brain getting fatigued with something, try switching to something different, perhaps every 15-30 minutes.

Another approach is to continue reading the same book, just move on to the next objective, and follow the same reading pattern that we just went through for the first objective. You can continue this until one of two things happens. Either you start to get mentally tired of so much new material, or the new objective requires a thorough understanding of the previous objective. Either way, it won't be very productive to keep going.

So you've read this particular section a couple of times. The key is to return to this section again and again, each time gaining more and more understanding. Each time you do this, repeat the pre-reading basic steps. Check your syllabus, outline, and objective. Skim the section you are about to read. Don't neglect this. Don't think, "I've already done this." This isn't about DOING; it's about UNDERSTANDING. If you simply fall back into the pattern of just reading, then you're just going to get the same old results. These little, extra steps I'm talking about are helping your brain get ready to understand by activating those parts of your brain that are needed to process and store the new information. This is one of the keys to getting more done in less time.

In addition to repetitive readings, in just a moment we'll talk about *taking notes* as you read. Furthermore, it's also important to keep in mind that this strategy assumes that other things are happening between these repetitive readings: lectures, assignments, quizzes, labs, activities, videos, discussions with other students, tutoring sessions. Learning complex concepts frequently requires multiple methods of input. Your reading will be most effective if you see this master plan at work. Keep your focus on the *learning objectives* and approach every one of these non-reading activities as an additional opportunity to make progress towards achieving them.

Hey, I know this is getting long. But any time you are in

serious trouble, you need some serious help. You don't need someone just saying, "Read it till you get it!" You need detailed instructions. If you are feeling a bit overwhelmed by all that I am telling you, then practice these strategies right now! Take a break and then come back and reread. Make sure you understand what I have said so far before proceeding to the next strategy (G). So either take a break (if you are feeling mentally full), or let's keep going.

G. Taking book notes

So let's talk about taking notes while you read as we continue to lay down the details for good reading comprehension. This is going to be another big section, so take your time. So... You're beginning a new chapter and you have:

1. Checked the syllabus.

2. Skimmed the whole chapter.

3. Made a brief outline of the chapter.

4. Listed the objectives for the chapter.

5. Identified the first objective.

6. Identified the pages that cover the first objective.

7. Quickly read that section, focused on what was understandable.

8. Read the section again, immediately, in order to reinforce what you understood.

9. Let some time go by (1-24 hours).

Now, you are ready for step **10**: read the section carefully *and take notes*. WOW! Really? Ten steps? Yes, and that is why this strategy is going to be so much more effective than trying to do everything at once. Look at all the mental preparation that is happening. This combination of reading the same material several times with different purposes and different methods is very powerful. Furthermore, the more you use this strategy, the better your brain will get at using it.

All right then. Let's begin with one comment on **how** to take notes, before we take a detailed look at **what** to take. Be BRIEF, yet thorough, by using abbreviations, symbols and phrases. Be organized. Use a helpful format like indenting, using all CAPS, underlining and/or highlighting. Write well enough so you can read it later, but don't get obsessed with neatness, and don't spend excessive amounts of time. Your goal is not to have this beautiful notebook that takes hours and hours to do. Don't spend loads of time copying notes just to make them look neater. Remember, time is limited. You can't do everything; you can't know everything. Don't spend hours and hours making a neat notebook and then complain that you are lost in a class. Now while it can be worthwhile to make a neat, organized notebook, provided you are processing the information as you reorganize, simplify, and make the notes easier to study from; mindless copying without engaging your brain won't profit you much. Your time is valuable. Always try to put your best effort where it will help you *learn* the most.

(NOTE: I have more ideas about taking notes in the next chapter when we look at classroom lectures. Some of those ideas could easily apply to your textbook as well.)

OK, let's talk about *what kind* of notes you will be taking during step 10. First of all, let's keep our mind focused on the purpose of all of this: TO LEARN. Therefore, keep asking yourself, "Are these notes helping me learn? Is there something I could be doing differently that might work better? Is there a faster way to do this?"

So let's make it clear. Why do we take notes? Have you ever thought about this? I mean really? And don't accept something like, "It helps me learn." Be specific. Why take notes? Well, let me give you some reasons.

1. It helps you focus while you read.

2. It uses more parts of your brain.

3. It keeps you more alert.

4. It sends a message to your subconscious that this is Funny, Aesthetic, Valuable, Odd, Rare, Important, Terrific, Exciting, or Special. (More about this in Chapter 5)

5. It forces you to process the material, not just look at it. It forces you to actually understand what you are reading, not just have the words pass before your eyes.

6. It creates a powerful review tool for later studying.

7. It creates a condensed piece of reference material for years to come.

So the most important thing I can tell you about note taking is to clearly identify what you hope these notes will do for you. Don't just take any old notes and think that some specific learning outcome will be achieved. If you want to specifically accomplish something, you have to design your note taking to do just that.

OK. So WHAT do you write?

I would begin by noting the date, the page in the book and the learning objective (using abbrs. of course). I would consider my purposes. I wouldn't write down a lot of stuff that I realize I already know. I would only want to remind myself of things I'm afraid I'll forget later. Personally, I would jot down notes in the same order as the items appear in the text and then later reorganize them if I want to. For example, I might write down vocab words (perhaps underlining them) along with everything else. Then later, make a separate list of the words I know I need extra practice on. Of course, you may choose to put the vocab in a separate section immediately and not include them in your general notes.

I mentioned it in strategy E a little while back, but let me say it again now. DON'T COPY! When taking book notes, you will learn more if you summarize, restate, explain things in your own way. This is why I am encouraging you to read a section several times before you begin writing.

To begin memorizing facts, one approach during step 10 is to write down any facts that you think will be on a test (e.g., the date for an event in history or a vocab term), AS YOU COME ACROSS THEM WHILE YOU ARE READING. *HOWEVER,* an even more effective approach is to scan the section and list the key facts BEFORE YOU START READING, *AND* WITHOUT ALL THE DETAILS. For example, write only the vocab term and leave space to fill in the definition later.

I suggest that when you do step 10 that you read and take notes for a section as follows:

1. Write the objective for the section.

2. Scan ahead and write a list of facts you will need to know (vocab, people's names, dates, etc.).

3. Read the section carefully (without writing) with the goal of achieving the objective and remembering the facts.

4. When finished reading the section, without looking at your book, see if you can write a summary of the key concept contained in the objective.

5. See if you can write in the details for each fact you have listed. For example, fill in the definition of a vocab term. And as always, AVOID COPYING.

6. Reread any portions as needed to accomplish numbers 4 and 5 above.

Continue this process through the chapter as time allows, one objective at a time. If during this process you notice that you are going to be memorizing a *lot* of data, you might want to have a plan for how you could organize (or *re*organize) all of this required knowledge. For example, in addition to your section-by-section notes, you might have a separate page, notebook section, or even an entirely different notebook, where you list all of the facts that you need to memorize. You might organize the data into a chart. You might make flash cards. You might make a database on your computer.

So let me summarize. There are two major types of notes you should be taking: details and concepts. Be sure to have some way to clearly distinguish these (use a highlighter, underline, indent, etc.). The details should be listed in some meaningful way that will make it easy for you to review this information frequently. When it comes to concepts, your goal is to summarize, in *your own words*, the major point of each section. And the big idea is to do all of this *without* copying. The more you make your brain work, the more it will remember and comprehend. (Again, I have more note-taking ideas in the next chapter on taking lecture notes.)

Organize Your Notes. Here's another idea that will help you get the most out of your note taking. Get a BIG PICTURE for how you want to organize your notes. This will take some practice. Ask around. Take a look at how other good students do their notebooks. Using a 3-ring binder might be a good idea. It makes it much easier to take notes on separate sheets of paper and then place them in the proper section, and in the proper order. As one possible example, you might have a separate section (or even notebook) for:

1. Book notes
2. Vocabulary
3. Facts to memorize
4. Lecture notes
5. Review notes

Also notice that while you may have invested some extra time up until now, you should start to see the payback at this point. For example, the better you understand what you are reading, the easier it will be to make concise, meaningful notes. You may also find yourself writing *less*. When you don't understand, you often find yourself writing everything and end up copying a lot. You think you're saving time by reading the chapter only once, and taking notes while you read. But.... you end up highlighting almost every line in your book, and almost rewriting the entire chapter in your notes. And in the end, spending a ton of time. And... learning very little.

One other important tip. As you are trying to understand what you read, if you have questions that you would like to ask the instructor, be sure to make a note of it. You might simply put a big question mark (especially in a different color) in the margin. You might want to have a separate page for questions. You might use a brightly colored sticky note. Then, when you get a chance, get the help you need. We all know what it's like to remember we had a question, but we can't remember what the question was. Let me also suggest that whenever you ask a question, you make it specific and detailed; you'll get a better answer that way. Show the teacher your notes. Show them an example of what you are having trouble with. Ask for another example. Ask for an analogy. Show them the spot in the book where you don't understand something. And if the answer they give you doesn't make sense right away, try again in a day or two. Learning is a process, and complicated subjects take time to learn. And try to keep in mind that it takes a lot longer to explain all of this, than it does to actually put it all into practice.

WOW! This is a lot to digest, so you might want to take a break. When you come back, scan the main points that we have already covered, then press ahead.

H. Work ahead of the instructor

I can't tell you how big this is! This is the difference between building a house with hand tools and power tools. Have you ever pounded a nail with a hammer, or put in a screw with a screwdriver? It takes many times longer by hand than with power tools. Working ahead of the instructor is just as powerful. It also makes going to class something to look forward to, instead of something to dread.

Now I know all instructors are unique, but in general it isn't too hard to know what they are going to do next. Usually you can look at a course outline or syllabus and see what's on today's agenda. Some teachers put a class calendar on the board or online. Some make specific announcements in class. So make a concerted effort to figure out what you need to do to always stay informed about what will be happening the next time you go to class. Therefore, try to do all 10 steps in Section G *before* you hear the lecture on the same topic(s).

So here's the trick. When you work ahead, you *don't* have to try to totally *understand* the new material. Instead, your reading and studying is done with this thought in mind: "What do I already know and understand in this section?" That way, you walk into class confident of what you already know, and with your ears primed to focus in on those items that you need to work on! This is also going to help you immensely with your lecture notes (and save you a lot of time too). More about that in the next chapter.

I. Read again, after class

Again, I know this list is getting long, but what makes this approach so powerful is that it gives your brain a chance to process the same information *many* times, with time in-between, during which your brain is creating new neural connections needed to comprehend and retain the new information.

So you just sat through a lecture. Now what? ASAP scan your notes and clean them up as needed. This should only take a few minutes, right after class. All you are doing is quickly scanning your lecture notes to be sure they are complete, accurate, and readable. Sometime later that same day, you have some study time set aside (not immediately, because we need to give our brain a chance to process what just happened).

Now ideally, the lecture you just sat through covered the same objective you've been reading about on your own. This is where you have to really be on top of your game. Your goal is to constantly coordinate your personal studying with what is happening in class so that they reinforce one another. The more you are able to do this, the more effective your studying will be.

So here is the basic cycle. Read about the objective several times and begin to take notes (steps 1-10). Hear about the objective (lecture) and add to those notes. Now, you want to use your textbook to *read* about the objective again, and adjust your notes as needed. The goal is to fine-tune this cycle to the degree that your understanding is growing at the same pace as the material is being covered in class, and to do this in the least amount of time as possible.

Now I know that you may be thinking that what I have been describing is going to take an enormous amount of time. But trust me. While that may be somewhat true at first, once you get in the habit, what you will find yourself doing is a lot of *little* steps, such that the *total* amount of time will end up being the same as (*or even less than*) what you have been doing in the past. But the BIG benefit is the amount of learning that you will be doing. In fact, even if it does end up taking a little more time, the reward in the learning (both quantity and quality) will be so worth it.

Therefore, what should happen during this post-lecture reread? Well, imagine what is happening inside your brain. Let me emphasize again that our minds work best when we work from the known to the unknown. THIS IS HUGE!!!!! This is why we always review what we know before we press ahead into new material. This is why we read something several times. We always want to establish a firm base of what we currently know and understand. Then, upon that foundation, we can add new facts, increase our understanding, and build new concepts. Furthermore, we need to continually reinforce this new material.

So by now, hopefully you have gotten past thinking, "But I've already read this once... twice... three times... etc." If you really want to learn something, then you can never read the same thing too many times. Every time you read the same thing, you will reinforce the material, your understanding will grow, and you will see new things that you missed before.

During these multiple readings, keep asking yourself, "Do I understand this? Does this make sense?" Also, from time to time, *stop reading*, if need be, and simply THINK! I can't stress this enough! One reason we may not understand what we are reading is because we just keep on reading!!! We don't take the time to stop and think about what we have just read, to let it soak in, to make sense of it all.

In other words, as you are studying, *take time to think*. Here are some ways to do this. Reread key sentences. Carefully examine charts, graphs and pictures. Try to answer any questions you find in the book. Work on a related assignment. Try to think of specific examples that further illustrate the main concept. Think of an experience in your life that this concept helps you understand better. See if you can explain *out loud* (and with pen and paper if possible) the main concept, while including as many details as you can. The more parts of your brain that you can engage (talking, listening, writing), the faster you will learn.

Now when these deeper insights hit you, and you finally understand a concept that made no sense before, when you finally get it, I personally want to welcome you to *The Higher Level Thinking Club of the World*. (I just made that up, lol.) But really, it's a wonderful experience that many people seldom enjoy. And keep in mind this saying: "The bigger the mountain, the better the view." No matter how big the challenge, our approach is to attack it in a lot of little pieces, until we can climb even the tallest of mountains.

Finally, it is very important to take the time to write down a summary of what you have just learned. (Remember to use abbrs. so you can do this quickly.) This is part of what will help lock it into your mind. However, because this is a new concept that you are learning, it will still need to be reviewed a few times to insure that you don't lose it. And writing things down will make it easier, and faster to do that. Therefore, try to write your summary in an easy-to-review format.

(NOTE: If the concept you are working on hasn't made sense by now, that doesn't mean that it never will. Hang in there. Don't give up. There are still many more helpful strategies to come.)

OK, time to move on.

(Or take a break and let this sink in!)

J. Read the end of chapter review

So you work your way through the chapter, day by day. You read ahead, you go to class, you read again. You read ahead, you go to class, you read again. You read ahead, until... You get to the end of the chapter.

EXTRA! EXTRA!

READ ALL ABOUT IT!!

WATCH OUT!!!

Check your course syllabus. You've just sat through the last lecture on the chapter. Your brain could really use some processing time. But be on your guard. Many instructors will have the test the very next day!! This is another reason why these reading strategies are so important. You need to be memorizing and understanding *as the chapter is being covered.* So why do so many people wait? And just look at the predicament they're in. How can they possibly learn the whole chapter in one day? And the answer is: THEY CAN'T!

The night before a test is NOT the time to be trying to memorize and understand the ENTIRE chapter. Instead, most of that work should already be done. The day before a test is the time to be *reviewing* recent material, not studying it for the first time.

So you've been dissecting the chapter, one concept at a time. You've been memorizing specific pieces of data. Now you need to step back and try to see the big picture. Put it all together. One great way to do this is to carefully read the chapter summary (if your book has one). Another great way is to do the next point (K).

K. Reread the entire chapter

"Man!! If I read this chapter one more time…
I'm gonna be an expert on it!!" EXACTLY!!

Now if you're thinking, "I don't have time to do all these steps," then take a few moments to add it all up and compare it to what you have been doing. Then compare the results, keeping in mind, it's not just about the input, it's about the output. And likewise, try to realize that when you work on small items, you can do them faster.

So even though you are reading and studying a greater *number* of times, the *amount* of time *per session* is smaller. And the really big time-saver is the night before the big test. While others are pouring caffeine into their bodies until the wee hours of the morning, trying to cram all that info into their head, only to end up with a poor test grade, and no long-term storage of all that material; you will be happily and healthfully spending only a very short time REVIEWING what you have already learned!! And you will walk into the test rested, relaxed and confident. Is this all starting to make sense?

So *how* should you read this chapter this one last time? Well, because of all the work you have already done, you should be able to read this chapter very fast. The purpose? First, repetition is a big key to long-term memory. Second, reading all the pieces one after the other will give you a better grasp of the big picture of the chapter. This will allow you to better see relationships (i.e., major concepts) between the smaller points, facts and examples in the chapter. Third, you may pick up a few details that you missed. And fourth, this should be a major confidence booster. Remember just a few days ago when you first looked at the chapter? Can you believe how much you have learned since then? And this confidence can be a tremendous asset come test time.

WOW! You made it! Take a break, then come back later and read strategies A through K again, and keep coming back from time to time, as you put these strategies to work in your classes. Practice the strategies *in* this chapter *on* this chapter. Make it your goal to become an expert reader and learner.

CHAPTER 4

Prepare Your Lecture Notes
BEFORE Class Starts

The key to great lecture notes is not the notes themselves. The key is in how you coordinate those notes with the rest of your learning. So right there is one reason why many people don't take effective notes. To begin with, taking effective notes is like reading your book; you have to know *why* you are taking notes before you jot down the first letter. So let's approach this like we're reading your text. Here's the big picture first, then we'll slow down and look at some specifics.

A. Pre-Class Preparation. We covered this in the previous chapter. Always look ahead and try to read about the lecture topic BEFORE you hear about it in class.

B. In-Class Preparation. Do a quick repeat of step A (Pre-Class Preparation) while waiting for class to start: look at your notes, get your textbook open to the current topic, get ready to take notes.

C. Focus and take good lecture notes. More about this in just a minute.

D. End-of-Class note check. After the lecture, take a couple of minutes to scan your notes for clarity and accuracy.

E. Study Time. Later that day, during your study time, use your lecture notes and the book to learn the material just covered.

F. Work ahead of the instructor. This completes the cycle. Begin your Pre-Class Preparation (step A) for the next lecture.

So there's the big picture. Now let's slow down and look at some specifics.

Be prepared for class.

This is so simple and yet so powerful. Get to class a few minutes early, **EVERY DAY**. If the instructor is late, use that time to study. You wouldn't throw money in the trash, so why would you treat your time any different? So each day, you get out your notes and textbook and any other needed items, such as a calculator and pencil (which you make sure is sharpened) or pen (which you make sure is working). You get out any assignments and make sure they are ready to be handed in. You open your notes and your textbook to the appropriate pages. If you still have time, you scan over such items as your course syllabus, chapter outline, yesterday's notes, and any questions you wrote in your notes during your study time. You make sure you are totally ready to catch the very first word out of the instructor's mouth. And if you still have time, you might play a quick game of WHAT'S THE PROFESSOR GOING TO DO FIRST? (Note: if you are afraid of appearing a bit unsociable, you can pretty much do all of the above while carrying on a polite conversation with those around you. In other words, there is absolutely no excuse for why you shouldn't have your book open and be ready to take notes the second the instructor begins to speak.)

So let's take a moment to think about taking notes in the context of your overall learning strategy. Remember, professors are called that for a reason. For the most part, they simply profess what they know. It is up to you to plug their input into your overall learning plan. If you walk into class prepared, then you should have a pretty good idea of:

1. What you already know.

2. What is going to happen today.

3. Some questions that you have.

At each point in the lecture, try to have something you are looking for in the information that is being presented. In other words, just like reading your book, you have an objective in mind, a purpose, something you are trying to learn. This is a major point to always keep in mind. Keep asking yourself, "What is it that I should be learning from what is happening right now?"

Get Organized

I know that this can be very challenging for many people. But the main point here is to have a plan and then do it.

Start with something simple, like writing down today's date. You might be amazed how such a simple thing can come in handy when studying your notes.

Next, once you have prepared for class to begin (notes and book ready, review done), try to identify the purpose of today's class. Once again, you check the syllabus, outline, and your previous notes. Not a bad idea to just keep these types of materials in front of you at all times. Therefore, as you are listening to the instructor's opening comments, you can identify the purpose of today's lecture and make a note of it. (Be sure to always abbreviate or use symbols so you can go fast.)

Now that you have a clear idea of what is coming (My apologies to you for those instructors who like to keep you guessing.), you want to begin a search for those important things that you need to extract from today's notes. Listening to a lecture should be like a game of, "I know that, I didn't know that." In other words, part of what you hear should be review and part should be new. Now don't get bored or fall asleep during the parts that are review. Nor should you be furiously writing down every word you hear. Instead, use this as a time to make sure you properly understand everything as well as you think you do. Look for little things (like new examples) that will deepen your understanding, such as a better way to organize the information you are learning. This is also a good time to play, "What will the professor say next." Or, "I wonder if the professor ever makes a mistake?" Stay sharp. Use this time to reinforce what you are learning, to make sure you haven't learned something wrong, to be sure you haven't missed something, and to think more deeply about specific topics.

The bottom line is (By the way, why do we say, "the bottom line is"? Where did that come from?) you only need to write down information that helps you clarify old material or understand new material. (Or perhaps to emphasize: THIS WILL BE ON THE TEST!) And you only need to write what you know is not in the book. (And you know what's in the book because you've already looked at it, even if you didn't understand it.) Have your textbook open during a lecture and when the instructor refers to it directly (or even indirectly), make a note of the book's page number in your notes. That way, you don't have to write down a bunch of notes, just write, "read p. 95." Note taking should not be trying to copy down everything the instructor says. You want to spend more time listening, and thinking, and less time writing. This is all made possible because back in chapter 3 you learned how to read ahead.

Be brief. You can elaborate and rewrite notes later. But right now you're trying to keep up with the world's fastest talker. Don't try to write complete sentences. Leave out words. Write down just the key words and abbreviate them. Try not to simply copy, but summarize key points in your own words.

However, if the instructor is showing you how to solve a math related problem, this is probably a good time to copy everything they do. However, do your best to avoid *mindless* copying. Try to process the information as you copy it. Can you follow the logic? If you have a question, be brave and raise your hand. I would also suggest, that if you have time, do the calculation on your calculator to prove to yourself that you can get the same answer. And if you are allowed to use a calculator on the test (or a quiz), be sure to always use the same calculator, all the time, so that you are very familiar with what it can do and where all the keys are.

By the way, have you considered making an audio or video recording of the lecture? HOWEVER, ALWAYS CHECK WITH THE PROFESSOR FIRST. This might not be allowed.

Again, use lots of abbreviations. (Why is abbreviation such a long word?) Come up with a list of common abbreviations (Like abbr.!) for words you use, uh, commonly!

Make up an abbr. that makes sense within the context of the lecture. This is made easier by your pre-reading since you have an idea of what's coming and what's in your book. For example, while KE may make no sense out of context, within the context of a lecture on Kinetic Energy, it makes perfect sense.

Try writing without vowels. Or try writing just the first half of longer words. Or try using phonics (write the way a word sounds, not how it is really spelled).

Some suggestions for abbreviations.

w/ : with

fol : following

w/n : within

b4 : before

b/n : between

b/c : because

mem: memorize this

* : This is important

~ : approximately

= : equals, is the same as, like

: number

< : is less than, is less important

% : percent

> : is greater than, more important than

+ : and

Here are some other abbr. ideas.

1. Try writing without vowels.

     crfl = careful

2. Try writing just the first half of longer words.

     encyc = encyclopedia

3. Try using numbers as part of a word

     gr8 = great

     b4 = before

4. Try using phonics (the way a word sounds)

cuz = because

5. Use text message abbreviations.

6. Use shorter words or slang for bigger words.

Big	Instead of	Gigantic
Tiny	Instead of	microscopic
Psyche	Instead of	Psychology
Anat	Instead of	Anatomy
Lit	Instead of	Literature

Here are some more time saving tips.

Use your book. Use abbrs. used in the book. Refer to page numbers. For example, let's say you write p20 in your notes and then write "* KFC." When you review your notes you look for something important (*) that you need to know on page 20 in your text, and you see that the topic is the 3 temperature scales. So immediately you know what you meant by KFC (Kelvin, Fahrenheit and Celsius), not Kentucky Fried Chicken.

Take advantage of technology. Notes may be available on the Internet. You may be able to download a copy of your textbook onto your laptop. Can you take a digital picture of a chalkboard full of notes? Could you walk into class with today's lecture notes already in front of you on your laptop? Could you record an audio and/or video of the lecture and save it on your computer? BE SURE TO ALWAYS CHECK WITH THE PROFESSOR ABOUT THE USE OF TECHNOLOGY IN THE CLASSROOM.

Remember, we are trying to learn, no matter how we get our notes. And the physical process of taking the notes themselves can many times actually reduce learning. We are so busy writing, we miss a lot of what is said, not to mention all the visuals. The goal is not to have the notes; the goal is to learn. The notes should clarify complex topics for us, and help us focus on what is most important. Typically, whatever the instructor puts in their notes is a way of saying, "This is important." It probably also means, "This is on the test!"

Here's an idea if you have online instructor notes. Have those notes in front of you during class and modify them as you find helpful. For example, underline or make bold those things that are more important and/or are definitely going to be on a test. Add in additional examples given in class that are not in the notes. Add extra comments like:

Ask about this.   Know this.

See page ___ in the book.

You might find it works better to print these notes out on paper, then handwrite your modifications during class. Be aware that you might actually learn better by handwriting notes rather than typing them. As with any strategy, do a little experimenting, and find out what works best for you.

If you have certain comments that you use repeatedly (this is on the test), then make some symbols so you can enter them quickly. Or use an abbr. Or use one word, like TEST, to mean a phrase, "This is on the test." Or just use a big T.

Remember, during class we want to try our best to keep our focus on understanding what is being said and demonstrated. Our notes should be a way of reminding us what those items are without the process itself being a distraction, and therefore a hindrance to learning.

AS YOU CAN SEE, GOOD NOTE TAKING REQUIRES SOME PLANNING AHEAD AND SOME PRACTICE. DON'T GIVE UP JUST BECAUSE IT ISN'T EASY AT FIRST.

As a teacher, I am always impressed by those students who are actively engaged with me during class (eyes wide open, making eye contact with me, nodding their head in agreement) who take just a few notes DURING class because they are doing all the things we've been talking about. They enjoy the class. They get a lot out of it. Learning is exciting. Learning is fun. Even the most challenging of subjects, when approached properly, can be an enjoyable experience. I hope the ideas that I am sharing with you will help you achieve this.

IT'S GAME TIME!

WARNING. THIS IS NOT FOR BEGINNERS.

This is definitely only for those times when you are really on top of your game. You've had a lot of experience and success. In fact, you might even be getting a little bored in class. So what can you do when you feel like it might be time for you to take over for the instructor? It's time to play, WHAT'S THE TEACHER GONNA DO NEXT? Can you guess? What are they going to say next? What's the next example? Will they use the example in the book or will they make up one of their own? Do I feel a personal story coming, a demonstration, a question thrown out to the students? By the way, on a similar note, when you are reading your text, you can play, WHAT'S ON THE NEXT PAGE? This is also a really good review strategy. For example, see if you can scan the entire chapter in your mind, page by page, picture by picture, example by example, following your chapter outline, all without opening the book at all.

Hey, if this is all sounding like a bunch of work... well... it is! But hey, learning requires work. But here's the really good news. This starts to sound like a big, time consuming ordeal when you put it all down on paper at one time. But in practice, as you do it, as you get used to doing it, it actually starts to save you time. For example, you are learning to use the time you used to waste; and now, you're turning it into profit. Academic profit. In fact, academic investment. Why? Because new learning builds on previous learning. So the work you do this chapter will save you time in future chapters. Now that's worth getting excited about!!!!

After class studying and review.

OK. So you put forth your best effort to take good lecture notes. Now what? First, let me say congratulations for taking notes. Let me further say, that even if you never look at those notes, it is still to your advantage to take them. Why? Because by doing so, you do several important things that will help your brain process and retain some of that information. Perhaps the most important thing is that it sent a message to your subconscious that this class is important and this is the really important info that we need to know and understand. In addition, you use more parts of your brain in order to write (and read). And the more parts of your brain that are engaged in the learning process, the better the results. Note taking also helps you keep focused and alert. It's pretty easy to start to daydream, even fall asleep, if you're just staring into space.

But let's not be satisfied with just taking notes. Let's keep a good thing going. Shortly after taking these notes (and I do mean SHORTLY, as in ASAP, the sooner the better, immediately if possible) you will want to scan over them for two big reasons. *First*, check for accuracy. Did you write everything down correctly? Can you read your writing? Do you understand your abbr.? *Second*, make additions. Was there something you wanted to write down but ran out of time? Is there something you want to say more about in order to clarify your notes? Your notes may make perfect sense while the echoes of the instructor's voice are still in your head. But will they make sense a week from now? Make any adjustments and add any extra comments to make sure they do. If needed, fill in any words or letters that you left blank.

Note: The main point of this exercise is to make sure that your notes will be useful to you during your study time. Therefore, THIS IS NOT STUDY TIME. In other words, don't think to yourself, "I'll wait to check my notes when I have time to study them." By then, it may be too late. This means that this step should be a very brief one, maybe just a few minutes.

Furthermore, if you don't take a few moments right after the lecture to check the quality of your notes, then you may find that those notes can actually become a hindrance to good studying. Have you ever become frustrated when looking at your notes because you can't read them; they make no sense; they leave you confused? If this ever happens to you, let it be a sign that you need to improve your note-taking skills. Put these ideas I'm giving you into practice and see what happens. Get someone to help you. Talk to your instructor. Go to the school's academic resource center. Whatever you do, don't give up. Taking good notes is a skill that must be practiced and developed. Even once you know what to do, it will take time doing it in order for you to become really good at it.

Finally, when it comes time to study your notes, you may find it extremely helpful to rewrite your notes. You may want to use an entirely different notebook (or section) for this. This gives you the chance to put all the pieces together into one coherent study tool. Try not to just copy your notes neater. Instead, using your book, your reading notes, and your lecture notes, try organizing all the material you are learning into a concise, meaningful study guide. Remember to always avoid mindless copying. We always want to be processing the information, because that is what leads to better understanding and long-term results.

Chapter 5

Memorization Tips
and
Other Study Strategies

If you have read chapters 3 and 4, let's do a quick recap of the learning process. First, you do your best to prepare yourself BEFORE class (chapter 3). Then, you do your best to get as much out of class AS IT HAPPENS (chapter 4). And now, what do you do? Let's think of it this way. 100% represents all that you need to learn. During your *pre*-class preparation, let's say you realize that you already know about 10%. During class, your preparation and incomparable note-taking strategies allow you to comprehend another 10-30%. Now, your *post*-class studying has 2 objectives. First, to *understand* the remaining 60-80%. And second, to *reinforce* 100% of the material for long-term storage. Let's take each of these separately.

Part 1: Studying to *understand* NEW material

Here's one of the big time savers that comes from using the strategies found in chapters 3 and 4. Because of all the work you have already done, if you simply read the book carefully, book and lecture notes in hand, you might be amazed at how much of the new material will just come clear while you're reading. And keep in mind, it is not necessary to understand *everything* before you begin to commit some parts of it to long-term memory. In fact, there are some concepts which absolutely won't come clear, until AFTER you have acquired a large body of new facts, upon which such an understanding can be built.

But here's the secret! Just reading about those facts and knowing where they are located in the book is not the same as having them memorized. Why? Because having them memorized allows your subconscious to ponder them, to look for relationships, to search for the answers to questions that you have. Haven't you had this happen to you? You've been memorizing a bunch of data for some class and then suddenly, seemingly from out of nowhere, a flash of insight just pops into your brain, oftentimes at unpredictable moments. In fact, you may find that an evening focused on memorizing a plethora of facts is rewarded with a flash of insight the next morning after a restful night of sleep.

Let's add some more to what I just said, but from a different angle. As a general rule, begin by working on whatever is *easiest*. Memorizing a fact is easier than understanding a concept. Therefore, as you begin a new chapter, identify ASAP the easiest things that you need to know. You can begin working on these immediately, even if you don't understand how they relate to the bigger concepts.

And here's the magic of the mind. As you are consciously focused on learning facts, your subconscious will be preparing itself for the concepts!!! Isn't that awesome!! This will be even more the case if you have skimmed the chapter, read the objectives, made an outline, etc. (See chapter 3) All of these strategies that we have been looking at in chapters 3 and 4 will have the result of making your mind more ready and more able to quickly and thoroughly understand complex concepts.

Now, I know that understanding a concept is much more difficult than simply memorizing a bunch of facts. But when the going gets tough, please don't give in. It's OK to memorize in the beginning, but don't stop there. Don't be satisfied. Please take a moment to try and understand this very important point. The more you understand the current chapter you are studying, the easier it makes it to understand what is coming in future chapters. For example, in chemistry, understanding the atom helps you understand compounds, which helps you understand chemical reactions. But when you never understand the facts that you are memorizing, your brain can become overwhelmed with a mountain of meaningless information. The more nonsense you are memorizing, the more overwhelmed your brain can become. In other words, memorizing without understanding, can make it *more* difficult to memorize the next thing.

The point here is that comprehension of complex concepts is a process of many small steps. The goal of this book is to show you a wide variety of these smaller steps, so that you can figure out which ones help you get the bigger results that you are after. As you are doing this, try to keep in mind that if a lot of these learning strategies are new to you, you may find that at first they don't work as quickly as you would like. For example, the moment of understanding may hit a week after the test. But hey, at least it did come, and hopefully your semester exam grade will be the benefactor. In addition, many times, concepts build upon one another. Therefore, although your insight came slow, it will still help you as you are introduced to even bigger concepts.

But be encouraged that as you continually employ these strategies, your mind will get better and better at using them. Eventually, the understanding will come BEFORE the test. Eventually, you will be able to keep up with the pace of the course. And this is where things get really exciting, as each new concept enables you to more thoroughly and more quickly catch on to the next one!

This is the level at which learning becomes a thrilling, fulfilling experience. It is my hope that you will persevere until this happens for you. Some will find that this happens very quickly. Others may take years. No matter how fast your brain puts this all together, be encouraged. Every step of progress that you make, leaves you better off than you were before. Hang in there! You can make it!

Part 2: Studying to remember

So where are we now? On the one hand, there are certain

concepts which you are understanding quickly, which you now need to commit to long-term memory. At the same time, there are those concepts needing more work. In addition, you have a set of facts that you need to memorize for a quiz or test. Since concepts are built upon learned facts, let's focus our attention for the remainder of this chapter on the learning of basic information. This is so important. Just because you don't understand something the first time you hear about it, doesn't mean your situation is hopeless. Identify the most basic information and work your way up from there. Don't procrastinate. Time is both your best friend and your worst enemy. Put these *study smart strategies* to use ASAP. The more difficult something is, the more time you will need.

OK. It's time. I need to pause again for a little more brain theory.

Your conscious mind, the part you are using right now, is only a small part of your brain's total capabilities. Just think about all the stuff you know that you could recall if I asked you, "What is your address, phone number, etc.?" But even more than memory, just imagine what your brain must have to do to be able to read and write, to speak, to see, to play music, do sports, and on and on it goes. Even if you feel like a poor student, you have an incredibly powerful brain that can process more information faster than even the world's best computers. The fact that you can comprehend what I am writing puts you way ahead of any computer.

So how can we tap into this powerhouse? Well, it may help you to think of your brain like a factory with a lot of people working in it. One of those people is in charge of your *long-term* memory. But before your *long-term* memory "sentinel" can even get the chance to decide whether or not to store a piece of information, that item has to first pass the inspection of the person in charge of your *short-term* memory. So the first trick is to get the attention of your *short-term* memory. Without my writing pages and pages, here are some simple keys to keep in mind. Whatever the information is that you are trying to learn, ask yourself, is it...

F unny

A esthetic

V aluable

O dd

R are

I mportant

T errific

E xciting

S pecial

"FAVORITES" is what we call an acronym, like SCUBA (Self-Contained Underwater Breathing Apparatus).

Now here's the problem. Our brain gets flooded with so much information all the time, that it would be a waste of resources (using up memory space and slowing down processing) to try to remember and comprehend *everything* that it "sees." (Of course, input can come from any of the five senses, not just sight.) So our *short-term* memory is constantly doing two things. First, it is filtering out all of the background information. Second, it is retaining the non-background information in sort of a holding pattern, or RAM if you're thinking computers. This is like all the temporary information that will be lost if your computer suddenly loses power. Your *long-term* memory is more like your hard drive; it is much more permanent. But the trick is getting the information stored there. And to get it there, you have to go through your Short-Term Memory (STM).

So your first job is to get the STM to take notice of the information. (Did I already say that?) The second job is to get the STM to pass on the information to the LTM (Long-Term Memory). Fortunately, many of the very things that will get the attention of the STM are also part of what will get that information passed on to the LTM. So let me elaborate a bit on the list I gave you a minute ago.

To begin with, I'm sure you can think of examples where you have a specific memory that stands out in your mind because it fits one or more of the listed criteria. The classic example is a time when something very painful happened, such as getting burned or cut. But on a more pleasant note, how about something that took place in a classroom? What was it about that memory that makes it stick out in your mind? Was it funny? Strange? Well, it was probably something on this list.

So how do we put this list to use on a daily basis? Well, let me say that hopefully a lot of this happens quite naturally. For example, we have an instructor that just seems to make it easier for us to learn. Why? Because they are using the list (whether they know it or not). They have a way of making class interesting, funny, and unusual. And certainly there are things that come easier to you than others. Why? You guessed it, the list! There are certain things that you just naturally are drawn to, find interesting, enjoy, find humor in, etc.

So here is a really important tip. *Know thyself.* Go through the list and give examples of each item. What kinds of things are you interested in? What do you value? What strikes you as funny? What do you think is beautiful (aesthetic)? Keep watching yourself and keep adding to the list. The more examples you are aware of, the more learning tools you'll have to work with. Now along with adding to your list of examples, your next tip is to start putting that information to work for you. And here's how you do it.

As you are going through the steps I've been giving you (while you are reading, taking notes, or studying), start looking for ways that you could use one of your examples to get your STM to take notice of something that you want it to remember or understand. For example, as you are skimming a chapter, look for something funny. Make fun of your textbook. As you scan the pictures, look for things in the pictures that are high on your interest list. For example, look at the cars. What kind are they? What year are they? Look at the styles of clothing. What year do you think the picture was taken? Or how about looking for mistakes? Or what about simply asking why that picture is in this chapter? Or how about just reminding yourself, "This stuff is important! I need to do well in this class because _____ ."

Now in case this isn't making sense, let me approach it from the opposite side. Look at what a lot of people do when they look at a chapter. They stare like a zombie as they flip the boring pages, wishing they didn't have to read this stupid book. What message is that sending to their STM????

So here is some great news. There are many simple ways you can "trick" your STM into taking note of something. Here is a simple one. Think about how you act when you think something is Funny, Aesthetic, Valuable, Odd, Rare, Important, Terrific, Exciting, or Special. Now act that way when you read, take notes, or study.

Think about it this way. Your STM is watching you in order to decide if it should commit something to memory. So, what if this is what it sees? You stroll into class late, shuffling your feet, wishing you could be somewhere else. You plop down in your seat, slouch back like you are on the couch at home, and cross your arms. Your books are closed. You gaze at the boring instructor, again wishing you didn't have to be there. Do I need to continue?

Is this making sense? "You mean I really don't have to be interested in something in order to send the message to my STM that something is interesting, and therefore worthy of remembering?" Exactly! So let me clarify this. Even if you aren't all that interested in a class you're taking (maybe it's a required class), you can still get there early, get your books ready, sit forward in your chair, put a grin on your face, greet those around you, and be ready to take notes the minute class begins. All of this will send a message to your brain to get ready, something good is coming. In other words, go back to what you said about how you act when you think something is Funny, Aesthetic, Valuable, Odd, Rare, Important, Terrific, Exciting, or Special. Now act that way when go to class, read your book, or study for a test.

So let's continue. Now that you have the attention of your STM, what do you need to do to get it to pass the information on to your Long-Term Memory? Fortunately, the very things that got the attention of the STM are also part of what will get that information passed on to the LTM. (Did I say that before too?) So don't forget to make what you are learning: Funny, Aesthetic, Valuable, Odd, Rare, Important, Terrific, Exciting, or Special. The more you exaggerate these aspects and the more of them you combine, the greater impact you will have on your memory.

Now, let's add to this: *timing*. To be most efficient (this means getting the most accomplished in the least amount of time) we need to do some planning. When we begin to learn something brand new, we need a lot of practice, in short bursts, done frequently. So as an example, let's say you have to memorize a list of facts. Start small, just a few of the facts, not the whole list (unless it is a small list). Experts tell us that 7 is about the limit. Keep the list small enough so that it is easy to do. Practice (I'll talk about *how* in just a moment) for about a minute, then stop. Do something else. A few minutes later (5-30), practice again. Keep this up throughout the day. Don't let 60 minutes go by without practicing at least once. The next day, do the same thing. As the days go by, you should be able to increase the amount of time between practices. In other words, you practice fewer times per day.

Now let's insert more information. As you continue to practice the old data, you want to add to it new data. For example, you've been working on 7 items, but there are twenty on the list. So as you get comfortable with the first seven items, start adding more. Now there are many ways to do this. You might:

1. Add one at a time. Gradually making your practice list longer.

2. Work on a new group separate, then merge it with the old group.

3. Add more details to the first group.

4. Start with a smaller group, but with the details already included. Then add only one new item at a time, but with all of its details).

So here are three principles to keep in mind.

1. New learning requires frequent use at first, then less frequent later, followed by occasional use (in order not to lose what you have learned).

2. New learning takes longer if you don't understand the material. In other words, try not to just copy and repeat what you are trying to memorize. Instead, think about it. Try to make sense out of it. Is there some kind of pattern? If so, why? When it comes to vocabulary, try asking yourself (and maybe your teacher), "Why did they give this name to that thing?"

3. New learning is more efficient if it is connected directly to that which we already know (the more intentional and the more meaningful, the better). Therefore, make a very deliberate effort to think about how these new facts fit into the bigger picture of the concept at hand, the chapter in the book, the place in the course outline. This is *HUGE*. The ease of retrieval of memorized data is directly connected to how it is stored. Before you start storing new information, take a moment to put it in a good place where you can find it later. You do this by deliberately thinking about your course and chapter outline. Where do these new facts fit in? In what context will you want to be able to recall them? Repeat this process the first few times you are practicing something new. After a while, the brain will remember where the new data is and you won't have to keep reminding it.

OK, so I just started to talk about HOW. So let's keep going with that. But first, let me start with a warning. Always look for better ways to learn. Don't get proud. Don't think that you have arrived. Don't think, "I already know how to memorize." And please allow me to challenge you. Once you have found a strategy that works well for you, do you know WHY? The more you understand WHY something works well for your brain, the better you will be able to put that knowledge to good use to become an even more efficient learner.

So here are some ideas. Look them over and try one that you have never used before. Ask around and see if you can add to this list. Share with others what works well for you. By the way, many of the items in this list are called mnemonic devices (or memory tricks). But no matter what you call them, what matters is that you find things that work for you. So here we go.

Make a word.

Use the first letter of each item to make a word (real or made-up). The more meaningful the word, the better. For example, in French, most consonants at the end of words are not pronounced, except for the letters C, R, F and L, which happen to be the consonants in the word

CaReFuL. Isn't that cool! In science we learn that the Pressure times the Volume of a gas equals the Number of moles times a constant R times the Temperature. So we get a formula: $PV = nRT$ which many people remember by the made up word: Pivnert. The great lakes are HOMES: Huron, Ontario, Michigan, Erie, Superior.

Make a sentence or phrase.

One of the classics comes from music where people memorize that "Every Good Boy Does Fine" in order to remember the notes (E G B D F) on the lines of sheet music. (They use F A C E for the spaces.) Therefore, take the first letter of each word in a list and use it as the first letter for a word in your made up sentence. Or you can do short phrases, word combos, etc. Ask your teacher. Each subject usually has its classics. In electrochemistry: **Red**uction occurs at the **Cat**hode = **Red Cats**. And **Ox**idation occurs at the **An**ode = **An Ox.** Likewise, **OIL RIG** = **O**xidation **I**s **L**oss of electrons, **R**eduction **I**s **G**ain of electrons.

Use Vocab parts.

Get in the habit of dissecting words. Learn common prefixes, suffixes, and roots. Make connections to words you already know. Throw in a little humor when you can. Make up stuff if you need to. My favorite example is the word chromosome. This is where your genes are located in the nucleus of a cell. *Chromo-* means **color**, and *-some* means **body**. So think of some other words that have *chromo-* in them and why: Chrome, Chromium,

Chromatophore, Chromosphere. And words that have -*some*: Ribosome, Lysosome. And throw in some humor. The suffix -*some* means **body**, cause <u>every</u> <u>body</u> wants to be *Some Body!*!! (Be sure to throw in a good accent in your voice.) Then add some meaning. Why are chromosomes called *colored bodies*? You might think that it is because they contain the genes (not jeans) that determine what color your body is. But the real reason goes back to when biologists first learned how to stain cells, so that they could see what they were made of. Guess which part was one of the first to take on a color, and therefore appeared as a *colored body*?

Take a walk.

Picture a place (room, house, town, countryside, park, etc.). Then imagine yourself taking a virtual trip. As you make your way around the scene, picture objects that help you remember the items in your list. And don't forget to make things: Funny, Aesthetic, Valuable, Odd, Rare, Important, Terrific, Exciting, or Special. Similar ideas would include painting a mental picture, making a story or a song. If you really like this idea, you might look into a book that explains it in detail.

Drill.

Rapid Repetition. For example, using flash cards. With any strategy, repetition is one of the big keys to getting something to stick. On the one hand, the more powerful your strategy, the less repetition will be needed. Conversely, you can memorize anything if you repeat it often enough. So what can you do to make *repetition* as efficient as possible? When you repeat what you are trying to memorize, use as many different modes of sensory input and output as possible, especially the ones that are your natural strengths.

This means, in as much as possible, process new information in as many ways as you can:

use it

say it

read it

sing it

taste it

draw it

write it

touch it

smell it

watch it

act it out

listen to it

experiment with it

feel it (emotionally)

say it in another language

talk to someone else about it

apply it to another area of learning

Now, you can't do all of these all of the time. And some of these will be much more effective for you than others. But let me suggest a very simple, yet powerful combination. The next time you are trying to memorize something, don't just stare at it. OH, BEWARE!! DON'T STARE TO PREPARE!! Instead... Look at it, speak it, listen to yourself speak it, and write it (at first you will be copying, eventually you will be doing it without looking at the original). If you prefer, sing it instead of saying it. And if you like, throw in a dance, or other choreographed movements, even something as simple as counting the items with your fingers.

So as an example, let's say you are trying to memorize some new facts, such as dates and events in history. Instead of just looking at your notes, copy your notes and say out loud what you are copying. As always, I would suggest using a lot of abbreviations so that this goes fast. Try writing the information down, while speaking it, 5 times in a row as quickly as you can.

Name, Date, Event

Armstrong, 1969, 1st on moon

Then go to the next item and do the same. Go through your list and then repeat this process several times a day. As the new items start to stick, you won't have to do each one as many times. And don't feel like you have to write things down *every* time you practice. And if all you can do is look at your flashcards, well that is certainly better than doing nothing.

The point is, when you practice, each additional part of your brain that you put into action will increase the rate and depth of your learning. Furthermore, each person will have certain modes of learning which are stronger. In other words, some people learn better by listening, others by watching, and others by doing. I would suggest that you take advantage of your natural strengths.

Now you may be forced to work on your weaknesses (such as having to listen to a lecture when you are stronger visually). Therefore, don't neglect your weaknesses, but it's OK to rely heavily upon your strengths; that's what strengths are for. Therefore, experiment and find out which ways of processing new information work the best for you. Then use those strategies to your advantage. (And don't be afraid to read a book or ask someone for help in order to figure out what your strengths are.)

And here's another tip. When you are in a situation where the primary mode of input is not your strength (you are listening to a lecture and you are a visual learner), then work hard at finding ways to put your strength to use. For example, *watch* the person carefully. Focus on any *diagrams* they might draw. Try to make a mental *picture* of what they are talking about and *draw* it in your notes. In other words, look for a way to translate the information from a mode of weakness to one of strength. For example, put the words you are hearing to music. Picture yourself actually doing what they are talking about; even make subtle, non-distracting finger or hand motions. If you are a good listener, then just listening carefully may be all you need to do. Likewise, you may not want to look at the person very much, just listen and take notes. Focus on what you are hearing and don't worry about looking at the person.

By the way, you might find it helpful (even important) that you clue in your instructor about what you are doing. For example, if you are a very visual person and find that you don't need to take a lot of notes during class, you might want to tell them. Otherwise, they may have a negative perspective on your lack of note taking. Likewise, if you get the feeling that your way of learning is not fitting in well with the instructor's teaching style, I would suggest you take the time to talk to them about this. Chances are you will find that this creates a much more pleasant classroom atmosphere.

And finally, if you need more help with memorizing information, you might look up a book on memory skills that focuses just on that.

HEY! Take a break. REALLY!

This is a good time to stop reading and let the previous section sink in. In other words, practice what you've been reading about. Remember, "Rome wasn't built in a day." And neither are good study skills and habits.

SECTION III

Putting Your Learning
to Good Use

In the previous section, I spent a lot of time talking about learning. Now let's turn our attention to the matter of getting good grades. As I do this, I'm going to use more of a college perspective, but many of my suggestions will work just as well in high school. And of course, if you are not in college yet, you will still want to be developing these college-level strategies (and habits) so that they are well developed by the time you do hit the college scene.

CHAPTER 6

Getting Good Grades on
Assignments, Papers, and other Projects

In order to learn well, you need to KNOW THYSELF. But in order to get good grades, you need to KNOW THY PROFESSOR!! Listen to how they talk. Watch what key points they stress. Try to see things from their point of view. Explain things the way they would explain them. Give them the answer you know that they think is the right answer. Show your work the way they show their work. In other words, until you have a really good reason to do otherwise, do things the way they do them. Give them what they want. Follow their directions exactly. Pay close attention to your syllabus. At the same time, let me encourage you *not* to lose sight of your learning strategies, as you go about the business of earning a good grade. My main piece of advice is to take a little time to think about how you can incorporate the required assignments into your overall study plan. With that said, let me make a few specific points.

DON'T COPY! We all know how little we learn when we just look up a vocabulary definition, copy an example, or skim the chapter just to find the answer to a question. Don't abandon your reading strategy. Instead, incorporate the assignment into it. For example, look at the questions, study the chapter, *then* do the assignment WITHOUT COPYING. For vocabulary words, identify where the assigned words are found in the chapter. Make it your goal to be able to define them AFTER you have studied that section. If you can't, go back and study the section again. And be sure to put the definitions in your own words. Also, add some examples to make the meaning more clear. Use both book examples (these might be on a test) and your own (these will quicken and deepen your understanding). Furthermore, if you have the option, format the assignment in a way that will make it easier to use it later as a study guide. For example, put a vertical line on the page and put the words on one side and the definitions on the other. This makes it easy to quiz yourself by covering up one side. And be sure to quiz yourself in BOTH directions. In the beginning, you will probably find it easier to always practice using the same pattern or sequence. But your goal should be to eventually do things in any order, at random, and in any direction. And once again, whenever possible, don't just stare to prepare. When you practice, say things out loud and write them down. (Remember all the learning strategies we covered in the previous chapter.)

PAPERS AND MAJOR PROJECTS.

GET STARTED ASAP!! The bigger and more difficult the assignment, the more important this will be. Keep EVERYTHING in perspective. Don't invest your whole life in a paper that is actually worth only a small percentage of your overall grade.

Woe to you Mr./Ms. PERFECTIONIST!! Keep your projects concise and on target. Do them like you do a test: get the main parts done, then go back and elaborate *if you have the time*. You might want to allocate how much time you can afford to put towards this project, keeping in mind all the other things on your calendar (and by all means, use a calendar or planner).

And above all else, make sure you refer to the project directions often and follow them exactly. Expect that your professors will tell you something only once. And watch out for professors that don't talk about an assignment in class because they explained it in the syllabus.

THE CREATIVE PROCESS IS A PROCESS. Good projects (such as research papers) often go through a time of refining. It's part of the creative process. You need time to gather information, verify facts, organize ideas, put things in writing, get new ideas, brainstorm, proof-read, rewrite, etc. This process can be fun and exciting, but it can also be hard, tedious, and stressful. One of the big keys is TIME. And here is some GREAT news! If you spread out these steps (put some time between them), then your subconscious will work on it for you, while your conscious is off doing something else (working, playing, even sleeping)! Ever have writer's block after hours of banging your head on your books? Then, take a nap, wake up, and every word just seems to fall into place? Hey, here's a great time (dare I say LIFE) saver. Always have a recording device handy. Whenever you have a sudden burst of insight (Brainstorm), record it. You might even want to have your recording tool handy by your bed or couch. Sometimes, people wake up with a new idea, only to lose it if they don't record it right away.

Furthermore, if you keep putting this project in front of your brain, then your brain will keep working on it for you. Let's say you've gathered your facts and you plan to do a lot of writing tonight. Then several times throughout the day, you glance at some of your notes. By the time you actually sit down to write, you'll probably have so many thoughts pouring out of your brain, you'll probably need some mind reading software to record it all. Well, seriously, you might want to have some voice recognition software.

At this point you begin a repeating cycle of brain-storming, recording, organizing and editing. When you get an idea (even if you know it's not a good one), just start writing. Let it rain. Once the storm is over, you can begin to organize and edit your thoughts. Don't be surprised if your final paper ends up a lot different than how it began. That's how the process often works. One thought leads to another and then another. And if you let this cycle repeat itself over a period of a few days, you'll probably be very happy with the result. Of course, if you wait till the night before the due date, well...

So, if you put a little time into planning your project, it will probably take less time, result in a better product, earn a better grade, and be more fun!! And oh yeah, produce more long-term learning!! Can you beat that?

Besides time, let's think a little more about content. If you have any power of choice in the selection of your topic, use it wisely. Choose topics that you think are Funny, Aesthetic, Valuable, Odd, Rare, Important, Terrific, Exciting, or Special (see chapter 5). And as you are researching your information (whether you got to choose the topic or not), look for facts that are Funny, Aesthetic, Valuable, Odd, Rare, Important, Terrific, Exciting, or Special. And as you brainstorm ideas, organize your project, and edit your writing, keep looking for things that are Funny, Aesthetic, Valuable, Odd, Rare, Important, Terrific, Exciting, or Special. (Are you getting the point that repetition is one of the keys to remembering something? ☺)

Finally, to really maximize your learning efficiency, look for topics and information that will reinforce the content you are covering in the lecture part of the course. (Hopefully, this is the professor's reason for assigning the project in the first place.) This can also be a great time to kill two birds with one stone. For example, what if you had to do an English paper, but you got to choose the topic? Why not choose a topic that puts to use information that you are learning in another class? Any chance you could use the same paper (or at least the topic) for two different classes? [Of course, check with your instructor(s) to see if this is allowed.]

MATH AND PROBLEM SOLVING.

Let's face it, math is different. And although a lot of the learning strategies in this book can be applied to any subject, math related courses present some unique challenges. This is why you may want to seek out your professor if you are in need of a lot of math related help. Furthermore, take advantage of every opportunity provided, such as special, problem solving sessions and math tutors. I have a math minor, have taught a number of math courses, and have taught a lot of chemistry (which incorporates a fair amount of math). So let me add a few simple math specific notes to all that I have already said.

Let's start with a brief comment about natural ability. There are those people who seem to pick up new math concepts very easily. On the other hand, there are those for whom my basic advice is to choose another major. (Yes, I actually said that!) The following notes are for those who fall somewhere in-between.

1. Start immediately. In high school the teacher may give you a lot of time in class to work. Don't expect that to be the case in college. Most, probably all, of your daily work will be done outside of class. You might even be tempted to skip some of this work because the professor might not even grade it! But you'll soon find out that it is probably pretty tough to pass the test without doing the homework. Therefore, don't procrastinate. You never know how much time you will need, so get started as soon after class as possible. If the assignments are in the syllabus, be sure to look ahead and get a head start if possible. And if math is not your favorite subject, it might be tempting to put it off until later, but you kind of know what is going to happen if you wait until late at night. If math is difficult for you, will it be any easier when you are tired?

2. Avoid doing it all at once. Sometimes a math assignment can contain a large number of very similar problems. After just a few questions, you might be in the zone and capable of quickly finishing the entire assignment. If that happens, be careful that you don't fall into **MINDLESS MATH MODE!!** Mindlessly following an example or a pattern is not what you are after. You want to understand the process and remember it for the long run. Therefore, let me suggest that you do enough of the assignment right after class so that you feel confident that you can do it. Then stop, and a little while later, continue. However, when you continue, I would suggest you first look over the book's explanation and example, the professor's explanation and example, and the first part of the assignment that you have already completed. Then, after you have successfully completed a few more problems, take another break. Repeat this process throughout the day until the assignment is done. And don't neglect the added benefit of saying out loud what you are thinking in your head. In other words, pretend you are explaining what your are doing to someone else, not just doing the homework for yourself. Once again, learning is a process. And the more ways we process the information, and the more time we give our brain to process that information, the better our results will be. In other words, working on your math for 30 minutes, four separate times throughout the day, will be much more beneficial than spending 2 hours all at once.

3. Study ahead. Just like you are going to read ahead, try doing some practice problems ahead. After you have completed the assignment that is due tomorrow, take a brief look ahead. Read the explanation and go through the sample problem(s) as much as you can. In fact, see if you can teach yourself. However, be careful! You don't want to practice doing something the wrong way. Don't start working ahead on an assignment, unless you are confident you are doing it correctly.

4. What if you are having TROUBLE? Now let's add to the steps above, what to do if you are NOT having quick success with daily work. This might also be suitable for problem sets for which you have several days to work on them before they are due. Here is one of the few cases where I am going to suggest that copying is a good strategy. But notice, I did *not* say mindless copying. If you are feeling a bit lost as to where to begin to solve a problem, try going back to a worked out example first. Look at your book or lecture notes. Look at a sample problem. See if you can follow the logic. Might I suggest that you say out loud what you are looking at? In other words, pretend you are the teacher walking the class through the solution. Then see if you can go through the solution yourself, WITHOUT the help of the book or your notes. If not, then COPY the work, WHILE SAYING IT OUT LOUD. In other words, don't just mindlessly copy it. Process it! Big Difference. Do this with as many examples as possible until you start to feel that you are getting the hang of it. Then, go back and see if you can redo one (or more) of the *same* examples, but this time *WITHOUT* LOOKING AT YOUR NOTES.

If this cyclical process does not produce immediate success, take a break. Give your subconscious mind some time to work. Switch over to some of your other classes, and then come back to this in an hour or two. Keep repeating this process with breaks in-between and get some extra help if necessary. You might see if there are any study groups on campus. And if you start to fall behind, do your best during the week, and then plan to put in some extra time on the weekend to get caught up. And if you are thinking of getting a tutor (many colleges provide these free of charge), that can be a great idea, provided they are not doing the work for you. Getting some one-on-one help could be just the thing you need to make all the pieces fall into place.

One more note. Don't underestimate the significance of doing a problem more than once. For example, start with the example the professor gave you in class. See if you can talk (out loud) your way through it. Then, talk your way through it again, but this time, copy it as you talk. A little while later, come back to it and see if you can talk and write the solution, but this time without copying. Anytime you get stuck, look at your notes, and continue copying and talking until you finish. Keep coming back to this problem again and again, until you can successfully go through the entire solution on your own.

5. Don't be a MAVERICK. Do your work the way THEY WANT IT. When it comes to your grade, I suggest that you play follow the leader. Follow their directions. Pay attention to any comments the professor makes in class about their expectations on assignments. Show your work the way they show their work. Be neat. Be organized. Number each question clearly (maybe put a circle around the number). Make the answer obvious (maybe put a rectangle around it). Leave a blank line between questions. Avoid clutter. Print clearly. Think of it this way: What thought do you want going through the professor's mind when they look at your paper?

Furthermore, I would be willing to argue that the more

clearly you show your work, the better you will be able to learn and remember what you are doing. For one thing, being neat and thorough makes it easier to spot and fix a mistake. It also makes it easier for someone else to help you. And, it will make it easier to use the assignment as a review tool, thereby saving you time, and probably increasing your scores on quizzes and tests. And finally, if you ever have to do any math as part of your future employment, how will your boss know that it was done right, unless they can clearly follow how you did it?

CHAPTER 7

Become a Quizzing Master

Quizzes usually require *short*-term learning strategies. But frequently, the point of a quiz is to help prepare you for a test, which requires more *long*-term learning strategies. Fortunately, you can usually accomplish both at the same time. So let's approach it that way. Quizzes are usually focused on a small body of facts or a single concept. Therefore, if you are looking ahead a little, it should be pretty easy to incorporate this small amount of material into your daily study routine. So here again we are saving time. Pay close attention to the memorization strategies we looked at in chapter 5. Remember to plan your learning strategy so that you avoid cramming. In fact, as soon as you take a test, immediately start working on the next chapter. If you start early, study in very short bursts (1-2 minutes), and do this several times a day for a few days, then not only will quiz taking be easier, but you should be committing this information to your *long*-term memory. Think of the time that you will save when you are reviewing for the test (or semester exam).

And think about this (THIS IS HUGE). Knowing this basic information should make understanding what is going on in class so much easier. So once again, plan ahead. I see it all the time. People who just cram for a quiz (or test) or do assignments as last minute busy work, seldom have a basic understanding of the concepts being covered in class. You will enjoy class so much more, if you incorporate all of your graded items into your daily study routine, with the goal of remembering and understanding the material for the *long* term. Approach all of your assignments as opportunities to learn, instead of busy work that you just have to get out of the way. Read ahead, start memorizing immediately, and anticipate each day's lecture, so when the next quiz "pops" up, you will be ready for it.

One additional note on quizzes. Try to find out what the format of the quiz will be. Then when you are studying the chapter, make up a practice quiz using the same format. So if you know that you will be writing a one paragraph explanation of something, actually practice writing out the explanation, don't just think about it. In addition, I would recommend saying it out loud while you write it. This uses more parts of your brain and will strengthen your memory. And by all means, DON'T COPY. Try to practice the quiz exactly as you will have to do it for real. The next chapter on studying for tests has some more ideas that might also be applicable to quizzes.

CHAPTER 8

How to *Practice* a Test
BEFORE You *Take* a Test

Doing poorly on tests is probably the most common problem students have. And many students are hoping for easy cures. And while there are some good *test-taking* strategies (see chapter 15), the most effective cure to poor test scores is improved *study* strategies and habits (section II). After all, the whole point of a test is to find out if you actually know and understand the material. Therefore, if you study effectively on a daily basis and arm yourself with a few simple test-taking strategies, you should see good results on test day. However, I do have some additional *study* tips specifically for tests.

Besides not knowing the material very well, I think that a major reason so many people do poorly on tests is that they don't practice test-like conditions. Imagine a musician who listened to the director, who looked at their music, who held their instrument, but never actually practiced playing the music. What could we expect out of their horn at the concert? Yet many people actually study this way, and then they wonder why they don't get better grades. Have you ever heard of pro football teams filling their practice fields with loud crowd noise? That's how they prepare for the real thing.

In other words, when you are studying for a test (or quiz),

don't just stare at your book or your notes. Instead, try practicing what you will have to do on "Game Day." This begins with doing your best to get a clear picture of what the test will look like. Check your course description, talk to students who have already taken the class, listen for clues given by the professor, and if you dare, ask the professor directly.

For starters, do your best to know what the test "rules" are. For example, how much time will you have? Will you be allowed to write on the test? Will scratch paper be allowed and/or provided? Knowing these "rules" will help you to better prepare. As an example, if you will have a place to write, think about preparing a "mental cheat sheet." In other words, what notes would you like to have in front of you while you are taking the test? Prepare this ahead of time (using abbreviations) and practice writing it out. Then on the day of the test, as soon as you get your test, write down these "notes." But be careful you don't use up too much of your allotted test time to do this. And you should definitely clear this with your instructor BEFORE the test day; you wouldn't want them to think that you were somehow cheating.

Next, let's talk about studying to get ready for different *kinds* of test questions.

ESSAY QUESTIONS

If you know ahead of time specific questions that will be asked, take the time to prepare a thorough answer. Check your notes and text. Write down your answer. Then reword it, being as succinct as possible, so that it will take very little test time to write a good answer. Then practice it. Practice it by writing it. In other words, practice like it's the real thing: no notes, limited time, no music, etc.

If you don't know the questions, use your intuition to make some logical guesses. And if you don't want to take the time to practice *writing* your answer, you could at least practice by saying it out loud. Either way, it is important to realize that even though you may feel like you understand something, that doesn't always mean that you can clearly communicate it? Writing out your answer (or at least talking it through) is a good way to prove to yourself that you can.

Now as much as I have been promoting the benefit of talking out loud, of course during the real test you'll have to be quiet. However, you could still mouth the words silently if you find that helps you. Just be sure you aren't actually saying the words or making any other distracting sounds or motions. By the way, this makes me think of a very important and special situation.

If you are aware that the testing environment has a significant impact on your ability to perform well, talk to your professor. Perhaps there is a special testing center on campus where you could be alone and talk out loud if you want. And if you have any kind of identified learning disability, be sure to advocate for any special helps that you need.

SHORT ANSWER QUESTIONS

If you know or suspect that you will have to do such things as list, describe, give examples or brief explanations, then make a list of possible questions and practice writing out the answers in the format that you suspect will be on the test.

SHOW WORK CALCULATIONS

Go back through your notes, assignments, and textbook and identify each type of problem. Then make a logical guess as to which types will be on the test. Next, look at an example of each question type, read the question, then close your eyes and visualize how you would go about solving it, then open your eyes and look at the work. Repeat this process until you can do every type of problem with ease. Probably a good idea to actually write out a few of the problems too, not just look at them. (More on this in a minute.)

OBJECTIVE QUESTIONS

Objective questions include Multiple Choice, True/False, Matching and Fill in. These can be hard to practice, but do your best to get your hands on some sample questions. Some teachers make previous tests available. Check out your textbook. Some books have suitable questions at the end of each section or chapter. Some textbooks have suitable questions at their web site. And even though the real test questions can frequently force you to think on your feet, you can still mentally prepare yourself by thinking like the teacher. As you review for the test, ask yourself what an objective question on this topic might look like.

Also, consider the content of most objective questions. For example:

1. Definition of vocabulary
2. Identify the name, date, place
3. Example of a concept or vocabulary term
4. Problem solving (calculation)
5. Recall of a fact

While there may be other formats that you encounter, the basic strategy remains the same. Practice. Do your best to know what is expected on the test and what format will be used. Then try to practice doing what you think you will have to do for real. In other words, if you are a poor test taker, then take more tests! The more you do anything, the better you'll get at it. Quit saying you're just a poor test taker and instead, start doing something about it. Ask your instructor if they have any old tests that you could practice with. You might suggest that you would self grade it so that it would cost them very little of their time. Also, see if you can retake a test, even if it doesn't change your grade.

And let me also add that during any of your studying, talking while you are writing can enhance your mental processing of the information and thus lead to better learning. Of course, as I mentioned before, just remember not to talk out loud during the real thing!

Finally, let me also suggest a very fast and effective way to study for a test using your assignments and any sample problems in your lecture notes. (I mentioned this briefly when talking about show work calculation questions.) Look at the question. Close your eyes and think about how to answer it (visualize it, verbalize it, even write it if you have the time and need the practice). Then look at your notes to verify the result. This helps you quickly practice the decision making process. It also helps the brain practice finding the saved information. It also breeds confidence because you are covering familiar ground. If you only do things once (read the chapter one time, do a homework problem one time), then everything is always new and different. Your mind never gets comfortable with the information. Think of all the songs that you know. How many times have you heard them? Remember that repetition is one of your memory's best friends. And a confident attitude can have a very positive effect on your test taking. And going back through your homework can breed a lot of confidence.

In closing, in this chapter I tried to stay focused on strategies related to STUDYING for tests and quizzes. In chapter 15, I will have more to say about this as I shift my focus to strategies for TAKING tests and quizzes. Therefore, you might find it helpful to skip ahead to chapter 15 right now.

CHAPTER 9

Let's ACE Our Semester Exams!

Well, here we are at the end of the road. And boy do I have great news! If you have been working hard every day, all semester, then there should be no need for cramming for your final exam!! I remember when I was in college, how a lot of the campus was going crazy at exam time. And I couldn't help but think that they were blind to the truth. Some seemed so proud of themselves that they had pulled an "all-nighter." On the other hand, my day of studying was pretty much like any other day before a test. And guess who got the highest grade on most of his exams? And I can still hear all the bellyaching.

> "That was the toughest test I've ever taken."

> "That test was ridiculous."

> "I studied all night, and I still failed it."

> "I didn't have a clue."

Well, by now, you should understand why this happens. If you want to do well on a semester exam, then you have to start working hard from day 1. Getting an A on an exam is like having an undefeated sports season. Do you think championship athletes only practice hard the week before the championship game? C'mon!

The secret to getting an A on an exam is really no secret.

It requires hard work, the first day of the semester, and every day. While you can certainly become more efficient in your learning, there is no shortcut to academic success.

So the first step to doing well on your semester exam is to do well on your chapter tests (see Chapter 8). Next, learn from your mistakes. Take the time to go back over your tests and keep working on what you missed. And finally, every chapter, spend some time reviewing the most important things from every previous chapter. You might want to make a written list of these review items. If possible, you might want to retake your chapter tests. And by the way, this is also the way you lock these items into your *long*-term memory, hopefully, forever. There is an old saying: "If you don't use it, you'll lose it." Therefore, make a plan to build into your weekly study schedule some time to review items you haven't used in a while. Keeping this material fresh in your mind *throughout* the semester is a major way to reduce the time needed for studying at the *end* of the semester.

At this point, let's assume that you are nearing the end of the course, and that you have been putting to use a lot of what I've been describing to you in this book. Do I have any *additional* suggestions specifically for semester exams?

> (Again, I have a lot of test *taking* tips in chapter 15, but right now we are just talking about *studying*.)

Well, what makes final exams different than a normal

chapter test? There are two main things that come to my mind. First is the length of the exam. This, of course, is due to the large amount of material it encompasses. And second, is the fact that you have these large exams occurring simultaneously in all your classes.

Therefore, I have one major addition to all that I have said before, especially what I covered in the previous chapter (chapter 8) where I talked about practicing "game day" conditions. How do you develop the stamina to study a large amount of material for an extended period of time? Let me use an analogy. If you are trying to pull on an object and your right arm gets tired, what might you do? Switch to your left? And after a while, if both arms get fatigued? Push with your foot?

Well, let's use your brain the same way. Your brain has groups of nerves that tend to specialize. For example, certain parts of your brain specialize in doing math calculations, others, language. So here's the idea. After 15-30 minutes of intense work on studying for one exam, try switching to a very different subject. In other words, try to constantly vary the type of mental activity that you are doing. In this way, you will probably be able to sustain a much higher level of thinking for a much longer period of time. Likewise, you might try a short 5-minute break every 30 minutes or so. You might also want to write up a schedule.

And speaking of endurance, one of the worst things you could do is try to stay up extra late the night before the test (or several nights in a row). This is always a bad idea, especially if you are pouring your favorite keep-awake-drink into your body. What happens if your brain crashes the moment the exam begins? In fact, if you feel the need to do this, then you ought to be willing to consider the possibility that you may have done something during the semester that put you into this position. Think about your priorities and be willing to make some changes as you move forward. If you are willing to put in 5 hours of studying during the middle of the night, which will probably be rather unproductive, then why wouldn't you be willing to put in some extra time every week, during the day, when you are the most alert and productive?

And take care of your body. Feed your body in order to feed your brain. If your diet is poor, if you are tired a lot, if you don't get much exercise and/or sleep, well... Need I say more?

So as the end of the semester approaches, stay on the offensive. Do some reviewing every day. Put off some things until *after* your exams, in order to give yourself more time *before* the exams. Rehearse every memorized item one more time. If you can, go back over your chapter tests. Then get a good night's sleep the night before the exam. Dress nice. Get a good breakfast. Get to class early. Have a positive attitude. Do a few jumping jacks to get the blood moving. And give it the best effort you can. I think you'll be pleased with the results.

SECTION IV

Putting it All Together

In the previous chapters, I've talked about motivation (section I), studying to learn (section II), and getting good grades (section III). In the next chapter, I want to try to simplify all of that information into a brief list, minus most of the explanation. This provides a different way of looking at these strategies and habits that should hopefully help you make a plan that produces the kind of results that you are looking for.

CHAPTER 10

A Suggested Pattern for Daily Studying

Can I do it? Can I make a very simple list of EVERYTHING I've talked about? Well, I'm going to try. But keep in mind the exact details of every day will be different: what classes you have, tests, due dates, etc. And a big variable will be the difficulty and amount of new material you are trying to learn. Some sections in your book you may only have to read once, and you've got it. Others may take a couple of readings per day for a week or two.

Anyway, without a lot of the extra explanation and details, let's see if I can walk you through the basics of a typical semester, from first day to semester exam.

Before the first day of class

Get all your class materials (usually at the campus bookstore if you're in college).

Check online (look for announcements from your professors).

Ask other students for any inside info on your instructors.

Get to know your textbooks.

Read over any provided course handouts (e.g., syllabus, outline, etc.), e-mails, online info, etc.

Do a very fast read of the first chapter and begin your note taking.

On the first day of class

Get to class early and get prepared:

Calculator

Pen/pencil

Notebook open

Write today's date

Check the syllabus

Textbook open to today's topic

After class, clean up your notes.

Look over any additional class information that was handed out.

Begin to set up a daily and weekly schedule for yourself.

Begin your daily study routine

1. Check the syllabus (update your planner as needed).

2. Skim the whole chapter.

3. Make a brief outline of the chapter.

4. List the objectives for the chapter (using abbrs. of course).

5. Identify the first objective in the chapter.

6. Identify the pages that cover the first objective.

7. Quickly read that section, focusing on what makes sense.

8. Read the section again, reinforcing what you understand, and loading into your brain what you do not.

9. Give your subconscious time to ponder what you just read. For example: move on to the next objective, or switch to a different class, or go eat lunch, etc.

10. *Carefully* read the pages covering the first objective (that you read two times earlier in steps 7 and 8) *and take notes*. As you are doing this, you want to try to coordinate your personal studying of the book with the topic of each coming lecture. This won't always be easy to do. Get organized and start memorizing vocab and other details.

Go to class

Get to class early and begin your pre-class preparation routine.

Take good notes.

Immediately after class, clean up your notes.

Check your daily planner and continue your daily study routine. BE SURE to include some review from previous chapters EVERY DAY. Study the objectives covered in class that day (use your lecture notes, read your book, take more notes).

Always keep looking ahead. Read ahead (and take notes if possible).

Work on assignments, and practice for quizzes, as part of your study routine.

At the end of each chapter/unit

Read the entire chapter quickly, one more time.

Read the chapter summary.

Practice "Game Day" conditions as you study for the chapter test.

Throughout the semester

During every chapter, try to review the major material from as many of the previous chapters as you can.

Allow extra time for work on major assignments and projects.

Schedule extra study times for quizzes and tests.

At the end of the semester

2-4 weeks before the exam dates, plan some time every day to study for your exams.

24 hours before each exam, follow your normal pretest routine. (Get plenty of sleep, eat a good breakfast, etc.)

Take your final exams.

Take a vacation!! (Seriously! You deserve it.)

There, I did it. Hopefully, this brief listing of what we have covered in several chapters, helps you get a better idea of how all of these pieces can fit together into a comprehensive plan. And this should just be the starting point. As you put these strategies into practice, make it your goal to find the exact steps that work the best for you. Remember, there is no magic formula. *You are the magic!* Therefore, I hope that you can use these ideas to develop your own formula for success.

One *final* note: Don't allow assignments and other graded items to destroy your daily reading and studying routine. Schedule extra time for these items. Otherwise, you will tend to fall back into that typical pattern of short-term learning, trying to get good grades, cramming for tests, and therefore, not really learning all that much.

At this point I feel like wishing you good luck. But luck has very little to do with learning and earning good grades. So it is my sincere hope that you find some or all of this material helpful. And I wish you great success in your academic endeavors. May you never stop *learning how to learn!*

However, there is still one more aspect to all of this. And that leads me to the last few chapters of this book. So far, I've tried to focus primarily on the learning process; however, there is more to college than that. In the next section, I'm going to give you a bunch of practical tips that hopefully will enable you to navigate some of the complexities of the college landscape, so that you not only learn a lot, but you also get good grades, and have an enjoyable and rewarding experience.

SECTION V

Adjusting to College Life

One of the most important things you can do to get ready for college is to *learn how to learn.* This has been the main focus of the previous three sections. In the following pages, I have attempted to do two additional things. One, I have tried to apply the general learning process that we have been exploring to some of the specific situations you may face at the college level. And two, I have also added some specific tips that should help you have a smoother transition from high school to college life.

(NOTE: Even though I am using the word *college* throughout this book, the information and ideas that I am presenting should be applicable to any post-secondary educational setting.)

CHAPTER 11

Before You Leave Home

"It's the summer before I head off to college.

What should I be doing to be prepared?"

Get lots of CASH!!!!!!

Hey, it's true. College is expensive, in lots of ways. My main advice to you is to get lots of help. A good place to start is your high school counselor. Likewise, colleges have financial counselors that can help you. Contact their admissions department. Talk to a LOT of people. Get LOTS of input.

I'm no expert on financial aid, but please allow me to share a few ideas with you that might prove very valuable. From my own experience, I found that the most significant source of financial aid came from the school that I (or my son) went to. Winning a national scholarship competition is pretty unlikely, and can be very time consuming. However, I would highly recommend applying for all the possible scholarships available at your chosen school. Also, if you are still deciding where to go (or thinking about transferring), I would suggest that you apply to several colleges, not just one, and request a financial aid package from each one that you are accepted to. Private schools that cost a lot usually have a lot of financial aid. In-state public schools may not have much aid, but what they charge can be significantly lower. Where you go is a big decision. Do some research and shop around.

[NOTE: Although choosing your school is a huge topic, and way beyond the scope of this book, I do have one quick suggestion you might find useful. Besides looking at the majors and programs offered by a school, you might also want to look at the information they provide about their professors. Many schools will have faculty profiles on their website. If you have a specific area of interest, see if any of the professors share this same passion. Look at what they got their Ph.D. in. Look at what research they are currently doing. Look at their publications. Also, once you have a name, you might even want to do a general search on the Internet to see what else you can learn about them. The idea is: If you are really interested in studying a particular topic, why not go to a school that has one or more professors who are experts in that field?]

OK, back to finances. Now once a school has offered you some financial aid, don't assume that what is in that financial award letter is the final word. Respond to the letter (perhaps more than once), and ask if they have any additional funds. Don't be afraid to do this even after you have decided to attend that school. And you might even check again, a couple of weeks before school starts. Maybe the school still has some unclaimed scholarship money left over. Hey, an extra thousand dollars might let you get by without having to have a job. (Seriously, I did this more than once. And it worked!)

AND, BE SURE TO LOOK INTO THIS _**EVERY**_ YEAR. Check with your professors and department heads. A lot of scholarships are tied to specific majors. So once you have decided on a major, recheck the scholarship opportunities. You might even want to schedule a meeting with your financial aid counselor EVERY SEMESTER.

And by all means, keep informed about any requirements to maintain the scholarships that you have already been given. Some financial awards renew every semester or year, but *only* if you meet certain requirements (such as a minimum GPA).

What about working while in college? Well, first let me say, don't make this decision lightly. If you are going to do well in college, you will have to make time for a lot of studying. And good studying requires that you be wide awake. People who try to work and go to school, often find themselves studying late at night. How well can you study if you feel tired most of the time? And how much easier is it to get sick when you are not getting enough sleep?

However, if financially you feel that you just have to work, try to do it when you're not in school: during the summer, or between semesters, or during breaks. If you have to work during the school year, try to work Friday nights and Saturdays. Try to avoid having to work late at night the day before a demanding class schedule.

Also, if you have to work, choose your work carefully. Consider the time and money it will take to get to and from work. Work on campus if you can. Even better, work in your major. If you're in science, see if you can be a lab aide. Check with your professors and see if they need any office help. Ask around about other programs, like internships. For example, there are summertime opportunities where you can get paid to work in the same field as your major. You earn money, learn, and get valuable experience (which you can put on your resume!!). Hey, did you ever think about working at Yellowstone (or some other national park) during the summer? It's like getting a paid vacation (sort of). Search the Internet. Look over your finances and make a plan.

On the other side of the ledger, think about your expenses. The less you spend, the less you have to earn. Do you really need the expense of having a car? Lots of college students don't have a car on campus. In fact, those who do, may find themselves busy giving other people rides. Can you afford this time and expense? And what if your car needs repairs, gets damaged, or even stolen? Many campuses are very "walker" friendly, and many people find that using a car is a hassle. What if you can't find a parking place? And if you do have to get somewhere farther away, consider other forms of transportation, like the bus, metro or taxi.

Lastly, let's talk about loans a little bit. Again, this is something you are going to want to get some expert advice on. For starters, I would highly recommend scheduling some time with your parents, guardians, guidance counselors, financial aid advisors, etc. Having these people involved can make a world of difference.

In the late winter of your senior year in high school, you will want to fill out what is called the FAFSA (Free Application for Federal Student Aid). The federal government uses this to determine if you are eligible for any federal grants and low cost federal loans. Schools may also use this in determining your financial aid package. Grants are free money, so you will definitely want to accept those. As for loans, the contract terms for *federal government* loans are usually better (often, much better) than what you can get through *private companies*. You might also ask around about *student loan forgiveness programs*. All of this can get very complicated, so be sure to start early and get lots of advice. Take the time to educate yourself on this very important matter. Unfortunately, many students can't even begin college because they don't have the needed finances. Others get started, but have to quit for the same reason. And those that do graduate may find themselves with a mountain of debt that can hang over their life for many, many years.

But no matter how you are able to cover the cost of going to school, don't kid yourself. Learning requires time and effort. Please allow me to make this point one more time. You are going to need time, focus and energy in order to study, learn and do well in your classes. The more time you need to spend making money or worrying about your financial situation, the harder it will make being successful in your classes. Why spend thousands of dollars, and years of time, just to sleep your way through school because you're working late night after night, and then end up with a mountain of debt? Incredible opportunities await those who develop themselves through a quality education. Don't squander your chance for that quality education for just a few dollars an hour.

CHAPTER 12

Choosing Your Classes

Options. Options. Options.

The three most important words to remember when signing up for classes are: options, options, options. What I mean is... If you aren't completely sure about your future plans (and even if you are), make choices that will ultimately give you the most options. For example, keep a close eye on things like required courses for graduation, or for a particular major. These are good things to take when you're not sure what to take. Also, look down the road a little. Try to take classes that will fulfill multiple requirements. For example, a particular psychology class might qualify for part of a major in education, business, sociology, etc. Whereas, a different psychology class might not.

Register ASAP.

This is a major difference between high school and college. Typically, in college, the class schedule is set first, and *then* the students register. You might even register for a specific time that the class is offered (often called a section). And when the class is full, that's it. You may have to wait until the next semester (which might mess up your overall plan and delay your graduation). Of course not all schools do things the same way, but the point is, find out and don't wait.

Get to know thy academic advisor.

Don't be afraid of being a pest. See them on a frequent basis. The better they know you, the better their advice will be. And don't be afraid to get advice from lots of sources. Talk to all of your professors. Ask them what they see in you; it might surprise you. Ask about taking a career aptitude test to get a better idea of what kind of job or profession might be a good fit for you. And if you have any interest in the military, you might want to talk to a recruiter. Along with aptitude tests (as well as just good, friendly advice), the armed forces have a lot of college related programs that could be the answer to your financial worries.

But in the end, listen to the voice inside you. Get to know thyself. This is probably one of the biggest reasons for going to college. It is also the reason why they require you to take a wide variety of courses that you might not choose for yourself. Look at these required courses as a chance to explore not only the world around you, but also the world inside you. Try something new. Expand your horizons. Take a course that requires some travel.

And don't be too afraid to give yourself some time. Although you certainly want to try to avoid wasting time (and money!) taking a class that you don't really need, it may take some time for you to figure what you are going to do with your life. There's a reason why many of your electives take place *after* your sophomore year. Many people discover that they needed that first year or two to explore their strengths, their interests, their potential. Don't get over anxious about this, but don't put it out of your mind either. BALANCE!! What a key word to remember in life. Often the extremes of all or nothing should be avoided. Likewise, just randomly choosing a class is probably not a good idea either. And even when you get focused and decide upon a major/career, you may want to throw in a couple of one-credit electives just to add some variety (and fun) to your schedule. Can you believe I took one-credit classes in scuba diving, downhill skiing and bird watching? It's true!

So let me end this thought again with the words *balance* and *options*. Invest some time thinking about your future. Invest some time gathering information. And do your best to make choices which will keep your life in *balance*, and/or give you the most *options* as you move forward.

And speaking of moving forward... Let's say that you've just graduated from high school. Summer is almost over. It's time to pack the bags and head off to college. In the next couple of very short chapters, let's take a look at your first few days on campus.

CHAPTER 13

College Orientation

Your school will no doubt have some freshmen orientation activities. I would recommend that you do as much of this as possible. The more you can get settled in before classes actually start, the better prepared you'll be when they do. Have fun these first few days. It may be a little scary meeting lots of new people, but remember, they are probably a bit nervous too. Think of this as your chance to make a fresh start. Be all you want to be!

You're free! You're free! No more parents looking over your shoulder. No more siblings getting in your way. You are on your own. You can do what you want. And wow, look at all the choices, tailored just for people your age. And look at all the people your age. And look at how much free time you have.

WARNING! WARNING!! WARNING!!!

Beware. There are two main types of choices to be careful of. First are those choices that will lead you away from your main goal. Watch out that you don't overload yourself with activities that have little to do with your education in general, or more specifically, your chosen major or vocation. Your time might be better spent by complementing your education; for example, being in marching band if you are a music major, or joining a science club if you are a science major. On the other hand, there is a lot to be said for diversification. Sometimes you can suffer overload and burnout if you only focus on one subject, 24/7. Doing something that is different and fun can sometimes be a mental lifesaver.

Beware. The second warning has to do with the *number* of choices you will have. Watch out that you don't get involved in too many things. Quality is probably more important than quantity. Here's the danger. When you first start college, you may feel a huge vacuum in your life. Many of your prior responsibilities and time-fillers are gone. And when you look at your class schedule, you may find yourself in class just a few hours per day. What are you going to do with all that extra time? Trust me. Ease your way into your new life situation. Don't overload yourself too quickly. Start slow, and as the months pass by, you'll be in a much better position to gauge your amount of free time. Please allow me to make the following recommendation. Begin college by erring on the side of allowing too *much* time for studying, instead of too *little*. It will be much easier to cut back study time than it will be to back out of commitments you have made to other people.

I need to reemphasize this point. One of the great reasons for poor academic performance is lack of quality study time on a regular basis. During the first month of school, things will probably go pretty smooth, and you may think, "This isn't so bad." And then, as midterms hit, and especially as finals start to loom large, the picture can suddenly turn drastic. The stress meter goes off the chart as people begin to realize all that is coming due: enormous amounts of reading, huge research projects, major exams, etc. People start pulling "all-nighters" in a desperate attempt to catch up. As the semester nears an end, everything seems to happen at the same time. And it does! But a little careful planning can allow you to avoid a lot of this. Get your class schedules, outlines, syllabi (Or is it syllabuses? Both are in the dictionary.) as fast as possible, and set up a master calendar of major dates. Then add extra activities. Build your time commitments around your classes, not around your extra activities.

BALANCE! BALANCE!! BALANCE!!!

BALANCE is the key word. You want to get a good education. You want to decide upon a major and eventually a career. But you also want to develop your whole person. You need to address the needs of your entire self, not just your academic self. You need to socialize. You need to try out some new things (within reason of course). You need to have some fun.

But you need to learn how to do all of these things in **BALANCE** with one another. Make yourself set priorities and make yourself stick to them. Your academic goals will probably require more time and concentrated effort than many of the other goals you have. And at times, your academic goals may require you to sacrifice some of your other goals. This is why it is very helpful to use some type of a calendar or planner to help you see the big picture, and to keep yourself in balance. And by the way, if you are having trouble in this area, I'll bet there is some office on campus that specializes in helping students with this very part of their college life. If you need some help, get it.

CHAPTER 14

The First Day of Class

Can you believe it? Tomorrow is your first day of college! What an exciting moment. However, for many students it will be a day filled with, "Wow, what just happened?" or "That was sure different than I expected." and many other "revelations." But if you have read most of this book, the "surprises" should come as no surprise to you. What a great feeling that will be. So let's keep a good thing going and get ready to hit the ground running!

To start with, make sure you know where all your classes are located. And if you are on a big campus, you might want to figure out how much time you are going to need to get to each one. Back in chapter 10, we talked about being academically ready for your first day. Now, let's add to that a few practical details.

The night before the big day, get to bed at a decent hour. Set that alarm. Wake up early. Get a good breakfast. Allow plenty of time to get your stuff together and get to class early. I don't mean 30 minutes early. But certainly at least 5 minutes; 10 minutes wouldn't hurt either. Hey, you might even get a chance to greet the professor. And if your class has 300 students... What? 300 students??!!! That's right. Many freshman classes, especially at bigger schools, can be huge. Some lecture halls are two or more stories tall. If you get there late, you may not even be able to see the professor from up in the nose bleed section. You might end up watching the lecture on a TV monitor. And you're paying how much for this "front row" seat?

Now I wouldn't recommend trying to "impress" the instructor. That could backfire. Some professors feel that it is their job to put uppity freshmen *in their place*. Just get there plenty early, sit somewhere near the front and be polite, cheerful, respectful, and quiet. In fact, it might be best not to say anything at all for the first few days (or even weeks).

Avoid making a negative first impression. Stay calm. Socialize a little (maybe). But be more like a spy or army scout. Scope out the territory. Be very observant. Start the process of getting to know your professor by using indirect means: look at the room, their desk, their clothes, their briefcase, their notes, their hair... Do they look neat, organized... You certainly don't want to be overly judgmental based on external appearances. But let's face it; what we look like on the outside does say a lot about what is on the inside.

Be ready for class to begin. By that I mean, ready to take notes. Some professors may start the first class like you've already been there a couple of weeks. No introduction. No welcomes. Just BOOM, and they're right into a 50-minute, nonstop lecture. Therefore, do everything to get your books, course syllabus, online lecture notes, etc., ahead of time. Be looking for information on how to do this as soon as you have registered for your classes. Ask about this during your orientation. Read ahead. Take notes ahead. Go into that first day ready to play offense, not defense.

And finally, don't assume your college classes will be just like high school. Be ready for a lot of changes; including, how and when to talk. I bet a whole book could be written about just this one thing! Seriously. My quick advice? Speak softly and listen A LOT! And especially be careful how and when you address your professor. When you listen to upper classmen, you may hear them saying "prof" a lot (short for professor). But when you go up to ask your professor a question, you should probably begin with doctor (provided they have a Ph.D.). Again, watch and listen a lot. And when you do get up the nerve to speak, may I suggest that you error on the side of being overly respectful and polite. You wouldn't want to start your college career by being the example the professor uses to inform people of what *not* to say.

Better Safe Than Sorry !!

CHAPTER 15

How to Play
the
Classroom Game
and
WIN!!

The biggest game in college

is not a team sport.

WIN. That's the goal. You want to graduate. You want to graduate with a respectable GPA. You want to land a good job. You want to begin a successful career.

OK. Wait a minute. I can't talk like this. I'm a teacher. The goal isn't to get an A. The goal is to learn. It's all about education, not getting good grades. We want to learn the material.

All right, I understand all of that. In fact, one of the central themes of everything that I have written is that if you will focus on learning, the good grades should naturally follow. In fact, I believe that the number one thing you can do to get better grades is to learn the material. However, sometimes, there is more to getting good grades than just that. Let me explain.

Do I want you to develop good study habits that result in a deeper level of learning that will stick with you for the long term? Yes. Do I want you to be persistent and consistent in your effort to learn? Yes. Do I want you to focus more on thoroughly understanding the material, than simply getting an A? Of course. But what I don't want to have happen is this. I don't want you to put in all of that effort, but end up with a poor grade. Your grade is based on specific criteria (which is most likely spelled out in your course syllabus). Knowing these criteria is your first step towards ensuring that you earn the grade that you desire. Therefore, in addition to all that I have said to help you learn better, I also have a number of hints and suggestions that I think will be of great use to you in your effort to earn the highest grade possible.

OK. Quick word of caution here. I am about to pour it on. I mean "drown" you in a plethora of ideas. (Isn't plethora an awesome word!) If this starts to get overwhelming, stop, and take a break. Some of these points won't make much sense (you might even think I'm a bit crazy) until they start happening to you. Think of this as reference material, and come back to it again and again as you are facing some of these situations.

All right, let it pour!

KNOW THY PROFESSOR

How? Quickest way? Find someone who has already taken the same class you are about to take. This may be hard if it is your first semester, because you may not know anyone yet. But it will also be easy, because odds are lots of other people have had to take the same class. In fact, you might have met some of them during your orientation. And chances are, many of them will be eager to share their knowledge. Keep asking around until you find someone. Suggestion: Go to a local hangout and yell out loud, "Did anybody here take instructor _____'s freshman English class?" (Throw in an offer to buy them something from the local establishment.) Chances are you will spur on a rousing discussion of all the *things to watch out for.* Here are some things you might want to ask:

    A. What kind of tests do they give?

    B. Do they care about spelling and grammar?

    C. How should I prepare for their tests?

    D. What do I have to do to get an A?

[NOTE: You can also look for online resources to get this information, but don't believe everything you read, and be sure to consider the source.]

HAVE THICK SKIN

This means you may have to be a little tough. In other words, don't take things too personally, especially in the beginning. Some professors like to "test" their students, to see what they are made of. Treat this like a game at first. As you get to know what's going on, then you'll be able to relax and be more yourself.

TEST TAKING STRATEGIES

In sections II - IV of this book, I gave you a lot of information on studying for understanding so that you will do well on assignments and tests. But here, I want to talk about game winning strategies: getting the highest grade you can on a test.

1. Find out what kind of tests this instructor gives. Ask around campus. Listen for hints during class. Read the syllabus. If you're brave, you might even venture to ask the Prof. However, I wouldn't try this in front of the whole class; you might have better luck one on one.

2. Psychoanalyze your Prof. Get into their head. Try to think like they do. What kind of questions will they ask? What kind of answers will they like? You'll get better at this as time goes by. One very important thing to do is to go over your graded assignments and tests very carefully. Analyze them. Look for patterns. Look for style. With each test you should get better at predicting what the next test will look like and therefore, how to better prepare for it.

3. Go for points. Some professors will put point values next to the questions. If not, make a logical guess. One question on an entirely blank page is probably worth a lot more than a simple fill in the blank. Put your greatest effort into what will give you the most points. Don't put enormous amounts of effort into a question only worth one point, only to run out of time answering a question worth 20 points. If answering an essay or short answer question, be very succinct. Avoid lots of meaningless words that take time to write and earn you no points. Avoid repeating the question. Avoid full, elaborate sentences (Unless your Prof. has a thing about this. Try to find out before the test.). Get right to the point. Use diagrams, outlining, bulleting, numbering. Use abbreviations that you know will be obvious to the Prof. (Be careful not to overdo this.) Use key words (like new vocab words from the chapter). Get the main points down and go on. If you have time at the end of the test, come back and put in a few added "extras" if you like.

An important side note: Objective vs. Subjective tests and questions. Objective tests are usually more obvious about point values. For example, all the multiple choice questions are probably worth the same number of points. So an easy question is worth the same as a hard question. Therefore, be sure to get through the whole test, answering all the easier ones first. But a subjective test can be tougher to figure out. If point values are not given for each question, you'll have to do a little reasoning to decide where to put forth your greatest effort. Some clues might be:

A. How much space is provided for your answer?

B. How much was this point stressed in class?

C. How is the question stated? A briefer question is probably looking for a briefer answer. If the question gives specific things to include in your response, then include them and put a little more effort into them.

D. What kind of comments has your instructor made about test answers? Have they stressed complete sentences? Are they concerned with how well you express an idea, how thoroughly you understand a complex concept, or are they just looking for the basic facts?

As always, your basic strategy is to put your best effort, the greatest amount of time, into those items that will bring you the greatest reward in points. This way, as the testing period comes to a close and you run out of time, you may only lose a few points. On the other hand, if you end up with some extra time, then you can go back and pick up some of those little points that you passed by earlier. For example, go back and put a little extra into a long essay question, or answer that tough multiple choice question that you left blank.

4. Scan the whole test before you start. This is critical to making sure you put your best effort, your greatest amount of time, into those parts of the test that are worth the most points. There is no law that says you must start on page 1 or question 1. Also, a test may be so long that you simply won't have time to do everything. Just make sure you do what will get you the most points in the end. Keep in mind, some instructors design tests to be too long for anyone to finish.

5. Decide upon a strategy. Do as much of this as possible *before* the test day. What do you think will be on the test? What will be worth the most points? What will be the hardest (or easiest) part of the test? Get as much info as you can, and then *plan your strategy*. You'll get better at this with each test (especially if you take the time to analyze the success of your strategy when you get your test back). Here are some options to consider.

Some people like to get all of the easy stuff out of the way first, so that they know exactly how much time they have remaining to focus on the more difficult items. However, if there is something very difficult that you have worked hard to prepare for (and is worth a lot of points), you might want to do that first. For example, what if you have memorized a large body of information (lots of names and dates in history, the compounds in the Kreb's cycle, a lengthy explanation for an essay question)? You might want to get this out of the way so you don't forget it during the rest of the test. You don't want to blank out later. Sometimes a test can start to frustrate you, and when the big topic comes, you may have trouble thinking clearly and quickly (and you're getting stressed because time is running out).

If you are allowed to write on the test, or if you are provided with some scratch paper, give this idea a try. Once the test begins, write down things that you have memorized that you are afraid you might forget or get confused about during the test. You might need to check with the Prof. about this, just to be sure they are OK with it.

So let's say you have twenty names and dates to remember. Practice them over and over a few minutes before the test. Keep repeating them (silently in your head) as you are waiting for the test to be passed out. As soon as you get the test, write them down. (Of course, use some sort of abbreviation so you can write them down quickly; after all, you do have a test to take.) Then, as you take the test, you can refer to these "notes."

In other words, what notes would you like to have in front of you when you are taking the test? Well, memorize them, and then write them out as soon as you get the test. Again, be sure the Prof. is OK with this. You wouldn't want them to think you were cheating.

Also, I would suggest that you keep any scratch notes neat and organized (put the question number by it, draw a box around it) so that you can come back to them later, if you wish. Furthermore, when doing calculations, I would recommend that you show enough work (including formulas and units) so that it is very clear to you that you are doing things correctly. But I wouldn't do any more than is needed to achieve this confidence, so that I can do things as quickly as possible. And of course, abbreviate as much as possible. In short, try to be very mindful of balancing this need for both speed and accuracy.

And finally, when it comes to planning your strategy, please allow me make one more important comment about showing math related work. The principle is this: the more you write down, the less you have to do in your head. And the more time you spend trying to figure things out in your head, the more tired your brain will become. Think of your brain like a muscle. Can you lift a gallon of milk? Can you lift it 100 times in a row? Just like your muscles will tire, so will your brain. By showing your work thoroughly, you allow your brain to focus on just a small portion of the problem, instead of the whole thing. This will help your brain to run a mental marathon, instead just a short sprint. Hopefully you can see that this strategy will be even more important when it comes time for your semester exams.

6. Know the rules of the test. Be sure to follow all test directions. Also, be on guard for how the test will be graded. This may not always be made clear, and you may have to find out the hard way. (This is why you want to ask around campus, "How does this Prof. grade their tests?") For example:

A. Does spelling count?

B. How much work do I have to show?

C. Do I lose points for wrong answers on a multiple choice test? (i.e., should I guess?)

D. Do I get any points if my answer is partially right?

E. Do I have to label all my numbers?

F. Do I have to use certain units in my answers?

G. Are there certain things that are just understood to be part of a question (even though they are not written: such as, use complete sentences, use metric units, show all work)?

H. Are we allowed to use any notes, to use a calculator, what kind of calculator?

I. How much time do we have? Can we stay after class to finish?

7. Be the last one to turn in your test. Take every available minute. Go back and check over your work. It's easy to make simple mistakes. We marked A even when we knew the answer was B. We write a number down wrong. We skip over a question. Or sometimes, a question later in a test will clear up something we were uncertain about earlier on the test.

8. Let the test help you. Frequently a question will have to contain certain information which must be presented correctly in order to properly ask the question. Use this to your advantage. For example, in chemistry, if you are asked to write the name of a compound, the formula must be written correctly. Therefore, later if you are asked to write the formula for a given name, that previous question might be of some help. Always be looking for ways that the test itself can help you take the test. This is part of why scanning the test before you start is so important. However, be careful that you don't over think a question. Many times your first impression is the best. Therefore, don't change your original answer unless you're absolutely sure.

9. Watch your stress level. Some stress will help you. If you are a bit nervous, that's good. Good blood flow to the brain will help it work better. But if you get over anxious, watch out. Take a brief time-out (30 seconds). Close your eyes, slow your breathing, calm down, say something positive to yourself. Then sharpen your focus. By this I mean, concentrate on only a small portion of the test. Tell yourself to quit worrying about the other questions, just think about this one question. If a question is really bothering you, leave it for now, and come back to it later. Remember your overall test strategy and get back on course. And whatever you do, don't just give up and take as long as you want (causing you to run out of time). Don't abandon ship just because you ran into some rough weather. You want to keep the pressure on, just not as much. It's like driving a car. You want to drive as fast as you can, as long as you stay in control. If the car starts to swerve, just slow down a little, but keep on going. Don't pull over to the side and quit. Don't take your foot off the gas and coast. Instead, take a moment to regroup, then get back in the game. Remember, the goal is to get as many points as you can. Quit worrying about the final outcome. Just keep saying to yourself, "How many points can I get on this next item?"

10. Keep an eye on the clock. Keep assessing your strategy and make adjustments as needed, based on how much time you have left. If you need to, wear a watch. By the way, if you find it hard to concentrate for a long period of time (maybe the test period is 50 minutes long), plan ahead of time to take several mental breaks (maybe 30 seconds every 10-15 minutes). Also, you might consider when you "practice for game day" to do the same thing. In other words, study hard for the same length of time. Likewise, experiment with how often you need a brief break. Again, think of your brain like a muscle. If you let it rest once in a while, you will be much less likely to "cramp up."

11. Avoid learning by trial and error. I'm sure you'll pick up other ideas as the months and years go by. But of course, you don't have to wait that long. Find some other students that have gone before you and have succeeded, and get their ideas. Ask your instructor. Go to the academic assistance office on campus. At times you may feel like you are all alone in this, but you are not. Ask. Cry. Beg. Plead. Do whatever it takes to get help. Don't remain silent in your distress.

USING YOUR SYLLABUS

Constantly be looking ahead for upcoming test days, quizzes, assignment due dates, lecture topics. Always work ahead. Don't be caught off guard. Don't expect reminders when things are due. If something (like a report) is clearly explained in the syllabus, don't expect any explanation in class. Some people get behind because they keep waiting for the instructor to explain something, or "assign" the due date. Always assume that if it is in the syllabus, that's your explanation, that's your notice that something is due. Don't wait for the instructor to verbalize the same thing in class. In fact, their response might be, "Well, I put it in the syllabus, didn't I?"

Come to class with your assignments in "ready-to-turn-in" form. Don't come to class and go looking for a stapler. In fact, make sure you own a stapler. Double check all assignment directions. Make sure you have followed all of them exactly. Some instructors will not even accept it any other way. Others may take it, but give you a failing grade or a zero when they discover you didn't follow their directions.

Oh, and here's a REALLY BIG ONE!!! Be sure you know in advance what to do if you are sick, or have to miss class for some reason. Some professors don't believe in second chances. Some will require a doctor's note. There may also be a campus-wide policy on this matter, so check your student handbook.

RESPECT YOUR PROFESSOR'S TIME

Work things around their schedule, not yours. Most instructors will post office hours. Some will schedule personal appointments. Some will offer extra help sessions. Take advantage of these, but avoid asking the Prof. to make an exception to see you. Work within the system they set up. Also keep in mind that if you have problems, you will have a better chance of getting help if you go in right away, instead of waiting until the last minute. Professors are usually more willing to help *before* crunch time comes. But don't be a pest. Only go when you genuinely need help. And be careful you don't wear out your welcome. Also, don't try to get "buddy buddy" with the Prof. unless they let down their guard first. Find out what they expect to be called: professor, doctor, etc. When in doubt, error on the side of respect. When it comes to having a good relationship with your instructor, let them be in the driver's seat. Be a good listener. Learn as much as you can from them. Ask them for their advice and help. Don't try to impress them with all that you know. Let them draw that out of you. Over time, a healthy relationship with your professor can be one of your greatest assets.

Don't walk into class late. If you do, don't be noisy or otherwise draw attention to yourself. Try to sneak in if you can (without looking sneaky). By the way, watch out for professors that lock the door once class begins. In which case, I would never knock. But I wouldn't walk away either. I'd quietly sit outside and try to hear as much as I could. And if the Prof. is late, you might impress your friends by leaving, but you'll probably impress the Prof. by staying.

THINK LIKE A PROFESSOR

Be careful that you don't get so into what you are learning that you forget to earn the points you'll need to get the grade you want. Frequently ask yourself some questions like...

A. How will the professor grade this?

B. How many points is this worth?

C. Is this going to be on the test?

D. What would be a good test question for this topic?

145

E. What does the professor expect me to learn from this?

F. Is the way that I'm doing this assignment going to impress the professor?

And Oh Yes... What NOT to say or do. *Don't ever say:*

> Is there any extra credit? (Answer: You're not in grade school any more.)
>
> What's on the test? (Answer: Everything.)
>
> Do we need to know that? (Answer: Evil stare.)

If there is something that you just have to know, see if you can get someone else to ask it. Lol ☺. Well, actually, just be very careful what you ask, especially during class.

GIVE THEM WHAT THEY WANT

Listen to how they talk. Watch what key points they stress. Try to see things from their point of view. Explain things the way they would explain them. Give them the answer you know that they think is the right answer. Show your work the way they show their work. In other words, until you have really good reasons to do otherwise, do things the way they do them. The beginning of your college career is not a good time to be a rugged individualist. The time for that will come later. Establish a solid grade point first. Earn their respect. Then you can enjoy some creativity without risking your GPA.

YOU CAN'T KNOW IT ALL

YOU CAN'T DO IT ALL

Put your effort where it will earn you the most points. If you are a perfectionist, you're going to have to make some tough decisions. Ask yourself, "Is it really worth the hours and hours of extra studying just to get a 98% on a test instead of a 93%?" Have I mentioned BALANCE before? You may simply have too many tests and too many projects to do, making it impossible to do every item to the best of your ability. And some tests just cover so much material that even if you had a year, you couldn't be ready for every possible question. And don't forget, there are professors that pride themselves on making sure that no one ever gets a 100% on a test.

It's OK to set your sights on getting an A in a class. But don't get consumed with getting a 100% on everything. Don't assume there's something wrong with you just because you missed a question or lost a point for something. And don't think that the professor looks down on you because you missed 2 questions out of 100.

And, dare I say it? Don't shoot for straight A's either. By allowing yourself a little margin for error, you will be a much happier person. You will have much greater balance in your life. Have I mentioned BALANCE before? A practicing physician doesn't have to remember every little thing from every class they ever took in order to be a great doctor. And those things that you do miss, that you do need to know, you can always learn them later. Isn't that great!! Learning isn't a one shot deal. You can always learn more later.

Trying to be academically "perfect" can be *very* stressful. And furthermore, when it comes to getting a job, it might even be a disadvantage. There are many other character traits that employers will be looking for. Among these would be how well you get along with other people, and how well you handle setbacks. Therefore, some of the sacrifices that you may have to make in order to get that 4.0 GPA, may actually become a disadvantage. This brings up a very important point. On your way to getting a degree, be on the lookout for some career counseling too. This is yet another area where it will be helpful to get as much input as you can.

DON'T OFFEND THY PROFESSOR

Speak softly and carry a big pencil. You have one mouth and 2 ears; use them in that ratio. The more subjective your grade is, the more important this can be.

KNOW YOUR OPTIONS

Check the course description and syllabus. How is your grade computed? How important are quizzes, homework, etc.? Is late work accepted? If so, what is the penalty? Do you have any options on which assignments, or how many, you have to turn in?

Do this with all of your classes at the beginning of the term, then compare them. Which classes are more strict?

Which ones give you more flexibility? Which professors are more lenient, forgiving, understanding, sympathetic? Look at due dates and make a game plan. Write out a list of your priorities. Which items are the most important (because they will have the biggest impact on your grade)? Which items could you turn in early and get out of the way immediately?

By the way, keep track of your grades. Write them down if you like. If they are available online, make it a habit to check your grades on a regular basis. (By the way, every 10 minutes is *not* regular. Try not to get too obsessed with this. ☺) No matter how you go about doing this, make it a priority to always know how your grade is doing. For example, you wouldn't want to discover that you missed an A in a class because you forgot to turn something in.

WOW! THIS GOES ON AND ON!! And so it does. But surely, this should be more than enough to get you off to a great start. Remember, the number one thing you can do to improve your grades is to learn the material. And that is what most of this book has been about. However, there are times that you will find that college is a whole lot simpler and less stressful, if you just treat it like a game. Therefore, may I suggest that you make it your goal to learn how the game is played, and then play it to get the most points. And hopefully these tips will help you make a 3-point shot your very first time out on the floor. And who knows, maybe you'll even get a slam dunk or two!

SECTION VI

Closing Remarks

If you are reading this because you have read most of this book, I congratulate you. I admire your desire to become the best learner you can be. I admire your perseverance.

The mere fact that you are willing to work hard to learn is a big factor in why you will be successful. But we all know that hard work isn't always enough. Sometimes life is a game. I hope that you have found some useful ideas in this material that will help you learn better AND earn a higher GPA.

My final thought is to emphasize the fact that you are unique. Your contribution to society will be unique. And we need your contribution! We need the best that you have to offer.

And because you are unique, no doubt you have already discovered that not everything I have suggested will work well for you. People tend to have a preferred mode of learning. For example, some learn best through visual input. Others are more auditory. Still others prefer some type of hands on experience.

I hope that in some way, this book has helped you to discover those modes of learning that work the best for you. I hope that as you practice these *Study Smart Strategies*, you will find the right combination that produces the results that you are after. And likewise, I hope that you are able to make good use of the many college survival tips that I included. In closing, I hope that all of this information helps your educational experience to be successful, enjoyable, and rewarding.

Best wishes for a happy and prosperous future,

(Or, if you know anything about *Star Trek*, "Live Long and Prosper!! ")

Doug Stratton

Made in the USA
Monee, IL
01 December 2024

71522427R00094